THE FIELD OF THISTLES

THE FIELD OF THISTLES

Scotland's Past and Scotland's People

MONICA CLOUGH

ILLUSTRATIONS BY WILLIE RODGER

MACDONALD PUBLISHERS
EDINBURGH

Published by Macdonald Publishers, Edinburgh
Edgefield Road, Loanhead,
Midlothian EH20 9SY

ISBN 0 904265 96 X

Printed in Scotland by
Macdonald Printers, Edinburgh

Contents

Foreword

I FEEL STRONGLY that an outline history of Scotland for the general reader should deal with ordinary people as well as with the rulers and decision makers, and should give some idea of the people's beliefs and interests, their strong individuality and sometimes prickly independence. And so, with a faint recollection of Piers the Ploughman's 'Fair field full of folk' we have called this account

THE FIELD OF THISTLES

I have to acknowledge with gratitude a debt to Professor Eric Richards, Professor David Buchan and Dr A. C. Chitnis whose work first taught me how to look at Scotland. Also I, with all who enjoy Scottish history, owe deep debts to the modern historians; mine are in particular to Professor G. W. S. Barrow, Professor R. Mitchison, Professor T. C. Smout, Dr Bruce Lenman, and the other contributors to the *New History of Scotland*, and to the *Edinburgh History of Scotland*, and to Professor A. Slaven. Willie Rodger wishes to acknowledge with thanks the help he has received from the National Portrait Gallery of Scotland, and we are both grateful to Ruari and Antonia McLean for much informed good advice. I also acknowledge a debt to Jean Redpath whose recorded singing of Scots ballads, and her pertinent comments, have been a running accompaniment to the writing of this book, and to Elisabeth Neech for her help in the technical preparation of the text; both of us thank Jenny Carter who had the initial idea that Willie and I collaborated in this book. The collaboration has been close, and has given us great pleasure, which I hope will be shared by our readers.

I have to acknowledge permission to quote from Professor D. Thomson's *Introduction to Gaelic Poetry* (1974) for John Roy Stewart, and Iain Mac Ailein; and from Dr Alan Macquarrie and the Inverness Field Club for his translation of Muiredhach Albanach's poem in *The Middle Ages In the Highlands* (1981). The extract on p. 170 is taken from 'To Circumjack Cencrastus', by Hugh MacDiarmid, and is reprinted with the permission of Macmillan Publishing Company, from his Collected Poems (© Christopher Murray Grieve, 1948 & 1962). Finally we both thank our families for their tolerant encouragement.

Monica Clough
Dunblane

I

Earliest Times

THERE IS A very strong sense of national identity among the Scots, an identity which developed early in our past and has persisted since the day nearly three hundred years ago when the separate political identity of the country was extinguished and absorbed into Great Britain. Technically, the history of the country should cease at the point in May 1707 when the Act of Union of Parliaments came into being. That would deny the great contribution of the Scottish Enlightenment to eighteenth-century culture, to omit the Jacobite risings, the songs of Burns and the novels of Scott, the seminal thinking of Adam Smith and of James Watt and the quiet Scottish revolution of the Disruption. There should be no surprise that we have not drawn a line at 1707, though our treatment of events since then is selective.

What is more surprising is not that Scottish national consciousness survives so strongly, but that it developed as early as in any nation-state in medieval Europe. There were many factors against this. The geography of the country presents a series of formidable natural barriers: mountains with difficult passes, a great sweep of islands from Shetland and Orkney through the Hebrides, wide estuaries and rivers and isolated tracts of fertile ground surrounded by poorer lands which long ago were bog, forest or empty moorland. It is less than two hundred years since our ancestors travelled for preference by the stormy sea, because of the horrors of the unmade roads, and only for about the same time has the scenery been at all admired. The Victorians, after they had constructed a fine network of railways, could afford to enthuse about the land of glens and bens; until then travel was difficult or dangerous. The parish bounded most horizons.

Still more than the nature of the ground, the nature of the peoples might have made for disunity. What we now call Scots are of a very mixed ethnic background. Out of very differing strains of blood and strands of birthplace the Scotsman has evolved as recognizable, vocal, proudly conscious of being a Scot since the early Middle Ages. Why—and how?

The earliest men and women lived on the shore margins as the last Ice Age thaws receded from good land. It was a simple life, hunting and fishing and moving on, with few pressures. They had rough shelters, and made their goods from stone and bone and basketwork; few examples have survived. Perhaps five thousand years ago a new race of pastoral incomers came up from the south, a people who built splendid monuments to their dead, and who lived apparently peacefully with their neighbours, who were few. These folk have left us burial cairns, barrows and standing stones marking their sacred places on the uplands and coastlines of the land. Their little flint arrowheads and heavier stone axes can be found. At Killin in Perthshire there was an axe factory, where stone axes were made and polished for export all over the country. Most of these would have been used for the laborious felling of the fringes of the thick forests of Caledonia.

Perhaps another thousand years passed, and further waves of peoples reached Scotland, ultimately impelled by great upheavals in Central Asia. The newcomers used bronze and spoke a kind of Common Celtic. The Celts had settled over much of Europe: pastoral, swaggering and athletic, not given to life in cities as lived by Romans and Greeks, though fond of display, gold and jewels. They tamed and bred horses, had herds of cattle and fought from chariots or from horseback, using short swords and going naked into battle with their long fair hair tied back, showing little fear: they apparently believed in rebirth. As settlers from these great tribes spread over Scotland the character of the monuments changed. Because they believed that death was a transient thing, burial became far less important: warfare was the business of men. All over the land these prehistoric peoples built duns, brochs, crannogs, earth houses, and embanked and fortified homesteads in great variety. The names and the outlines of many of these are still with us. The Celts settled as rulers and apparently intermarried with the former inhabitants.

By the time the Romans marched north, in the first century AD, the flux of time had separated the northern peoples into the tribes the Romans called the painted men, the Picts, who differed from the southern tribes, the men of Strathclyde, Galloway and Lothian. The latter were more kin to the rest of the Roman province of Britain, and spoke a different Celtic tongue from the Picts, one much more like present-day Welsh. The men of southern Scotland were British, part of a mainstream tradition.

Picts, Britons and Romans

What kind of people the Picts were is hard to deduce. It is not even clear what they called themselves—'Picts' or painted people is an obvious nickname—and their language has disappeared. In their heyday Pictish kingdoms ran from the Pentland Hills to the Pentland Firth, and they had about five hundred years of influence. Almost all we know of the Picts now is derived from their carved stones and their metalwork, alive with sinuous lines and cryptic symbols of which the endless interlace of the immortal serpent is the most striking. When they became Christians they adapted their symbols. Surviving illuminated manuscripts such as the Book of Kells, possibly made on Iona and carried to

Roman cavalry defeating the natives

Ireland, carry Pictish decorative traditions well into the Christian era, as do their stone monuments. Of all the ethnic and political strains in Scotland the Pictish one is the most difficult to assess, though it is of great importance. Traces of Pictish inheritance customs still faintly survive—for example peerages in Scotland can be held and pass through a woman, though not in England. The Picts were matriarchal. The sites of their little farms, facing south and high above damp wooded valleys, still hold faintly Pictish names, beginning with Pett or Pit, as in Pitlochry. Not much has yet been learned through the excavation of their hill forts, and the bones of Christian Picts probably lie unrecognizable in the oldest kirkyards in Scotland. Most of our information comes from the Romans, who fought them. The northern frontier of Roman Britain was never wholly quiet, and its location altered with altering military fortunes. It was military occupation, not colonization, as further south.

The Romans were in Scotland for nearly three hundred years, far longer than is popularly believed. They have left marching camps, and permanent forts, roads, defences and harbours from the Borders north to the Moray Firth. The standard Roman fort, built anywhere between the Euphrates and the Tay by the efficient Roman army, shows here one characteristic that is unusual if not unique to Scottish examples: there are more deep ditches and banks round Scottish Roman forts. The Picts attacked by a frontal charge, swords drawn; 1500 years later the Highland troops of Montrose or Dundee were doing the same. Only in southern Scotland is there evidence of frontier settlements with civilian populations attached, though no civil town was built. Newstead, near Melrose (which the Romans called Trimontium after the triple-headed Eildon Hills) is the best known of these. The outlines of the purely military forts at Ardoch in Strathallan (the largest Roman camp in Britain), Birrens in Dumfriesshire and Lyne in Peeblesshire are plain to see, and all have deep ditches. The connecting roads and signal stations are harder to identify, but much still survives.

The first campaign in the north, giving the first firm dates in Scottish history, happens to be well reported, as it was waged by Agricola, a relative of the Roman historian Tacitus. Agricola fought his way up to the Forth, in AD 80; this was always a difficult crossing and a natural frontier, as the Forth remained a wide area of marshy lakes and deep bog. The Pictish stronghold of Dumyat dominates the crossing, presumably the centre of the tribe later called the Maeatae. Agricola turned south-west into Ayrshire. By AD 83 he was ready to go north, keeping to the coast, and his fleet kept station with his marching army, providing cover, supplies, and perhaps an escape if needed. Eventually in AD 84 he brought the Picts to a pitched battle somewhere in Aberdeenshire, by a mountain Tacitus called Mons Graupius, which may be Bennachie. The federation of Pictish tribes went down, defeated by the trained Roman army. Their leader Calgacus (The Swordsman) was reported to have said that the Romans 'made a desert and called it a victory'. This was Agricola's intention. His fleet sailed round, north through the Pentland Firth and through the Hebrides, and back to Strathclyde, where at

Dumbarton ('the fort of the Britons') he was back in friendly territory. The Britons of Strathclyde and Galloway, the Votadini who lived in the Lothians, and the Selgoviae of the central uplands, who lived in the thick forests of Selkirk, had opted for a quieter life as Roman allies, and got on with the work of sheep farming and raising a little grain.

Hadrian built his great wall about AD 120, a little south of the present border, and possibly as much to prevent the unruly Brigantes of Yorkshire from going north to join the Picts as to deter the Picts coming in to reinforce them. A successful attack had led to the destruction of Newstead and other forts a little earlier. It was not long before decisions were reversed and a second wall was built on the Forth-Clyde line, from Bridgeness to Old Kilpatrick. It was constructed about the year 143 by the Governor of Britain, Quintus Lollius Urbicus, under the orders of the Emperor Antoninus Pius—hence its name of the Antonine Wall. It was intended to be the final frontier, and was well sited and well built by detachments from all three of the legions stationed in Britain. Perhaps ten thousand men were stationed along its length, ready to muster if hostile forces attempted to force it.

Between 208 and 211 the Emperor Septimius Severus conducted a long campaign against uprisings in the north of Scotland about which we know very little. By the end of a relatively peaceful third century Rome itself was threatened by Gothic incursions and was beginning to withdraw from its more distant frontiers. Defence was left to locally recruited allies, setting the Votadini of Lothian to police the Picts and newly arrived Scots in the west. By the end of the fourth century Rome was also having another very different effect on local populations: Christian missionaries had arrived. One of the pieces of evidence still stands at the door of the kirk of Kirkmadrine, in the Ross of Galloway, a gravestone inscribed with the Christian Chi-Rho monogram and the names of three priests, Ides, Viventius and Mavorius. It has been there since the middle of the fifth century. The Roman military withdrew at the beginning of the fifth century, taking with them their exotic foreign troops, like the Boatmen of the Euphrates who shivered on the North Sea at Cramond, or the Tungrians and the men who flavoured their food with poppy-seed, coriander and figs, which were found at the Roman camp at Bearsden. The Dark Age began.

The Dark Age: Angles and Scots

The Angles and the Saxons came swarming ashore, land-hungry, from Low Germany. Some Saxon troops may have worked as late Roman auxiliaries. All along eastern Britain they fought the native Britons, beating them back to the west and occupying their good farm lands, where Anglian names are still thick on Scottish ground, from Berwick to Edinburgh. Somewhere, some time, King

Arthur fought. Swirling out of the thick mist of later legend it is possible to see the outline of a great military commander, heir to the last of the Roman order and successful in rallying the Britons in 12 great battles against the invading Anglo-Saxons. At least one of these battles was in Scotland, though the exact location of *Cat Coit Caledon* has long been lost. And Arthur ultimately failed, and the Angles ruled all the north-east of Britain. The Votadini of Roman days became known as Gododdin, their castles were at Edinburgh and Stirling, but they too went down at a battle at Dunpender, and their leader Cuneda took his shattered followers to join the other Britons still fighting in Wales. They took with them their songs, which is why the earliest Scots epic poem is preserved in old Welsh: 'The Gododdin', a song about the battles of the men of Lothian. Edwin of Northumbria ruled from the Forth to Yorkshire, with Arthur's Seat a memory at the gates of Anglian Edinburgh. Anglians were dominant but fairly thin on the ground, ruling from large timbered halls, and directing the British peasant farmers to carry on. Gradually these men adopted the language of the conquerors, forgetting their British tongue and speaking 'Inglis', which became one of the native tongues of what we now call Scotland.

Back in Roman times, perhaps in the fourth century, a small raiding party from northern Ireland had landed in Argyll. They were the Scotti, two brawling brothers called by tradition Fergus and Lorn or (by another version) Loarn and Oengus, each head of a small raiding party, and accompanied by their grandfather. They were joined by more small contingents, who came slipping up the seaways from Ulster, pausing in Galloway and the lower Clyde, and carving out the kingdom later called Dal Riata in Argyllshire. Their little kingdoms were served from the sea and their lords held strong duns overlooking good anchorages. All the details of their settlement have been overlaid by later tales and legends. They made an old Pictish fort at Dunadd their chief fortress. The Scots were Celtic like the Picts and Britons, but brought with them little of the distinctive culture of Ireland, preferring to adopt the pottery, the weaving and the wives of local inhabitants, and carrying on the cattle-raising—and raiding—traditions of their common Celtic forebears. They spoke Erse—Irish—and they and this language gradually dominated the language and culture of the Picts. Gaelic in the Dark Ages spread from Scottish centres and modern Gaelic derives from Erse, not from Pictish or British roots.

Round about 501 the death of 'Fergus, Lord of Dal Riata' is recorded, and thereafter there seems to have been a relatively peaceful time during which Fergus's grandsons Comgall and Gabran successively ruled. 'Ruled' perhaps is the wrong word, it is more likely that they were the effective heads of warrior bands who did not much concern themselves with the arts of peaceful administration. In 563 Cowall son of Comgall gave the overlordship of the isle of Iona to the priest Columba, who was kin to one of the royal families of Ireland. Columba was a good politician as well as a great missionary saint, his advice was sought on all sides, and he did much to establish Aedan son of Gabran as an orthodox ruler in the west. The frontier between the lands of the Picts and the lands of the Scots was the great mountain mass of Drum Alban, and the Picts themselves were divided into the northern and southern kingdoms by the eastern extension of the Grampians, the Mounth. Columba made a political journey to the court of the high king of the northern Picts, Brudei, near Inverness. His own ruler, Aedan, conducted many raids against his neighbours, British, Pictish and Anglian, and although he suffered some heavy defeats, notably in 604 at Degsastan, somewhere in Northumbria, he survived and died an old man.

Picts and missionaries

The history, parallel in time, of the Pictish kingdoms is even more difficult to unravel than the Scots' affairs; even fewer and less reliable documents exist, none are contemporary. Small kingdoms were loosely federated, and over-kings and high kings are listed for the Picts as well as the Scots. Some Pict and Scot kings were clearly related. Pictish inheritance went through the female, and it is possible that they practised exogamy; that is that the royal women married well outside their kin group, they married strangers by choice. This apparently gave good opportunity for Scotsmen to be accepted by Pictish royal circles. The other well-established Pictish custom was for rule to pass by tanistry, not necessarily in a direct line but to the most suitable male heir of royal blood. This legitimized bloodshed by brothers and cousins even more than the more general patrilineal system did, at the time.

Throughout these centuries of warfare there had been Christian influences at work. How much of the work of the Roman Christians of the Rheged, the area round the Solway and Galloway, survived the breakdown of Roman rule is not known, but Christians there were in Scotland, before the legions left. Whithorn in Galloway is the best-known centre now, and excavation has recently established new details of the monastery there, though the identity of the earliest known missionary-saint, Ninian, has not become any clearer.

All saints suffered from the accretion of later legends. Ninian probably went abroad to be educated, possibly to Rome and to the great teaching centre of St Martin of Tours; later history has it so, but there is no evidence. Dedications to Ninian and to Martin are found very early indeed, also a tradition of Ninian's wide travels in Pictland; he certainly must be counted one of the great missionaries of the Dark Ages. Patrick, the apostle of Ireland, was born in the kingdom of Strathclyde by his own account, at a date and place unknown. Columba, coming from Ireland, continued the same tradition of travel.

The early bishops ministered not to a geographic area but each to a tribe, or kingdom. The early monasteries were single cells grouped in a rough circle surrounded by an embankment, a pattern derived from the anchorites of Egypt. All the monks of a community were expected to travel and preach, and to work in the monastery fields. Columba and his Iona monastery are the best known, but there were many others in the field: Moluoc on Lismore, Maelrubha at

Applecross, Mungo in Glasgow, Blane in Bute and at Dunblane, all preaching to the west of Drum Alban. The conversion of the northern Picts came later, and is likely to have been the work of the Northumbrian missionaries. These derived ultimately from Iona, through the work of Cuthbert and Aidan. Lindisfarne (Holy Island) became the great centre of Northumbrian Christianity, and the combination of Scottish faith and linear design with the greater riches and a new passion for learning had a great flowering in Northumbria, particularly in carving and illumination. In 664 the Synod of Whitby attempted to bring unity into a bitter dispute about the dating of Easter, central point of the Christian faith. Most of the Celtic Church gave agreement, but in practice it was a long time before Roman observances were adopted by all the Celtic churches.

In spite of the spread of the Christian faith, it would be unrealistic to equate the work of brilliant missionaries with the total sanctity of their flocks. Violent acts, and mean ones, were not wiped out, and strong pagan undertones persisted up and down the land for hundreds of years more. With the coming of monks, however, it was possible to choose (for some men and women) the peaceful hard work of the cloister, and to become literate. Records began to be kept, though hardly any survive.

Warrior from the Lewis chess set

Earliest Times

Northmen: the Lochlannaich arrive

The events concerning the eighth-century rulers of the Picts and of the Scottish kingdom of Dal Riata are dark and difficult to follow, and very bloodstained. The wars of the day were more like expeditions in search of loot and plunder than for territorial gain, and the pattern was shaken up by the incursion of two new elements. The Anglians had consolidated their holding of eastern Britain, and were aggressive and still more than half pagan. The Northmen left Norway under the pressure of population on a narrow land, and the earliest arrivals were raiders, simply. And they raided churches when they could, for that was where the wealth of the community had been concentrated. A native chief in Shetland hid his treasure beneath the church floor (where it lay until 1958), demonstrating that a family could own 28 pieces of worked silver plate of great elegance. The raids were greatly feared. The seamanship of the Northmen gave them command of the northern seas, and very soon Northmen began to settle wherever their ships could make good landfall.

Attacks, and the settlement of Orkney and Shetland, began about the middle of the eighth century, and on the mainland from 792 onward. Archaeological evidence has been found, at the settlements of Jarlshof in Shetland and Buckquoy in Orkney, of Viking longhouses replacing the native Pictish dwellings, and the sagas of the Northmen give plenty of evidence of peaceful farming and fishing, weaving and sheep herding as well as of warfare. The wonderful wooden boats, supple in construction and easy for expert seamen to sail or row, gave the Northmen a new dimension; they were more mobile than any of the land-based peoples. Evidence of place names and sagas point to the complete occupation of Orkney and Shetland, quite heavy settlements in the Hebrides, and on the mainland of Caithness and Sutherland. In the east the frontier town of the Northmen was Dingwall. In the Northern Isles the inhabitants soon spoke Norn, and forgot the Pictish dialects, but in the rest of Loch Lann, as the Norse settlements were called, a mixture of Norn and Erse left a mark on the place names, but ended with a Gaelic-speaking population whose aristocracy claimed Norse descent, and used Norse baptismal names. Somerled Lord of the Isles is the archetype. There is a little evidence that the Norsemen quickly took native wives, and adopted Christianity from the time of their first settlements. One of the earls of Orkney became better known as St Magnus after an exemplary life as a ruler and a Christian. The cathedral at Kirkwall is named for him. The Northmen naturally did not confine themselves to settling in Scottish territory. The empty islands of the Faeroes and Iceland were subsequently colonized, partly by settlers from Lewis in the Hebrides, and Vikings had kin in Dublin and Cumbria, or joined raiding parties based on the Isle of Man. Viking incursions into Cumbria, and later settlements from the Hebrides at the expense of native British and Anglian elements, gave south-west Scotland its name of Galloway, the country of the Gall-Ghaidhil, the foreign Gael. The area called Galloway was more extensive in the Middle Ages than at present.

Kings of Alba and Scotia

Meantime, in the middle of the ninth century the interaction between Picts and Scots had produced the first joint king, Kenneth mac Alpin, a Scot who ruled the lands called Alba by the Picts and Scotia by the Scots, lying between the Moray Firth and the Forth and Clyde. He was crowned at Scone in Perthshire by the old rites of the Picts, the senior race. The eastern seaboard of Alba, from Moray to Fife, was very little troubled by raids of Northmen, though how Kenneth achieved this is not known. His successors were not so fortunate, and Viking raids were again common. The neighbours of Alba, or Scotia, were Strathclyde, by now a declining British kingdom that acknowledged the supremacy of the kings of Scotia, and Lothian on the south bank of the Forth, stretching down to the rest of Northumbria, an Anglian possession. In the north and to the south-west were the Lochlannaich, the men of Norse descent. In the old province of the northern Picts the local rulers were the Mormaers, all of them in succession proud, contentious and conservative: after 100 years they reappear as dominants in northern Alba.

The reigns of Kenneth II and Malcolm are a confused record of fighting, during which these kings alternately attacked the lords of Lothian and Northumbria, or protected them (for a consideration) against the renewed raids of the Northmen. About the time that the Northmen were driven from York in 954, the Earls of Northumbria gave up the town of Edinburgh to the Scots, retaining Dunbar and most of Lothian. By the end of the century the King of Scots is one of half a dozen rulers who attended the delayed coronation of Edgar, King of the English, at Chester. Edgar gave him the rest of Lothian, a province that his successor lost again. Malcolm II, who became king about the year 1005, ruled until 1034. At the battle of Carham in 1018 Malcolm finally secured Lothian down to the Tweed, for Scotia.

In practice the King of Scotia (or Alba) did not have much authority north of the Spey where the powerful Mormaers of Moray held sway. Malcolm's attempts to make his grandson Duncan his successor met with strong opposition from Moray where the rival claimant was Macbeth, son of Findlaech, who had overcome several blood feuds in his own connection. Eventually Macbeth and Duncan met in battle and Duncan was killed in 1041. Macbeth's claim to the throne of Alba was based on tanist rules, and on his wife Gruoch's good claim through the matrilineal system, illustrating Highland conservatism and pride in ancestry. At any rate Macbeth and his queen were accepted, and moved to Fife, the centre of the kingdom, where he ruled peaceably for 17 years. So confident was he of his right that he neglected the usual precaution of killing his competitors; Duncan's sons Malcolm and Donald Ban were allowed to go into exile. First with Siward, Earl of Northumbria and then with pious and occasionally muddled Edward of England, the Confessor, Malcolm learned foreign ways and plotted a return. Macbeth meantime went in pilgrimage to Rome in 1050 where he astonished the sophisticated by his generosity to the poor and by his Celtic swagger. His wife founded a priory in Fife, and an Irish annalist called Macbeth 'the generous king'.

Malcolm Ceanmhor

In the south Malcolm Ceanmhor ('Bighead' or 'Great Chief') waited until Edward the Confessor settled with him and his other powerful subjects, the sons of Earl Godwin, for a carve-up. Malcolm married Ingibjorg, daughter of the Norse Earl of Orkney, and seized back the throne of the Scots from the aging Macbeth Finlayson whom he killed in 1058. Malcolm's marriage had conciliated the fierce Northmen of his northern frontier, indeed with them as allies and Tostig, Earl Godwin's half-Danish son, as partner he made a bid for a big slice of England, Northumbria. It was to become a Viking kingdom, they planned. Tostig's able younger brother Harold defeated Tostig's northern ambitions outside York, only to be defeated himself three weeks later by the Norman Duke William at Hastings. Malcolm retired into the Scottish heartland, to see what would happen next.

What did happen was unexpected and disconcerting. Edward the Confessor's nephew and legal heir Edward the Atheling had died young, leaving a small family brought up in exile in Hungary. They came on a visit to Scotland, and Malcolm Ceanmhor, a grizzled veteran, widower and illiterate, fell in love. He married Margaret, the very pious and young Saxon princess, to a chorus of

Dunfermline

17

disapproval. The marriage in 1070 altered the course of Scots history. Before it, the English nobles and dissatisfied Normans had occasionally taken refuge with the King of the Scots, now they were encouraged to flock north. Margaret made them welcome and put them to work. When she and her husband died they left a kingdom conforming to the European norms of the eleventh century, with Benedictine monks in Dunfermline following Roman rule with precision, with Norman knights holding lands of the king and building their motte-and-bailey castles over the land and scribes writing charters in Norman-French. Margaret managed to persuade her devoted and somewhat barbaric husband to conform more with feudal Europe, and she educated her children. Naturally the king was not, except in pious legend, entirely guided by his good girl-wife, and he made five attempts to take Northumbria for Scotland. By 1072 King William, with the south of England secured, thought it time to campaign to the north; William of Normandy was impossible to withstand. At Abernethy in 1072 Malcolm did homage and swore fealty to William. Did he swear personal loyalty or did he make the kings of Scotland subordinate to England for all time? The arguments which arose lasted long.

King David, the Sair Sanct

After Malcolm Ceanmhor's death there was a confused period, when his brother, an elderly backwoodsman, Donald Ban, claimed the throne; then his son Duncan II (by Ingibjorg) and then three of Margaret's sons, Edgar, Alexander I, and David I held the throne. One of their sisters was married to Henry I of England, and the links with England were close. Of these kings only King David—Queen Margaret's favourite youngest son—needs our special notice. He was well educated and later was called a 'sair sanct for the crown'; certainly he was devout. The kingdom was held together by kinship, chiefship, power, rights and obligations. The rules were Norman, such as were then being worked out from Orkney to the Norman Kingdom of Sicily, and eventually to Jerusalem itself, and the court mainly spoke French. King David gave his mind to justice, to the church and to military organization. He founded monasteries. He introduced his own coinage in Scotland, the first minted since the Romans withdrew.

His feeling for the more civilized world of Europe led him to give the first town charters, creating the royal burghs of Edinburgh, Roxburgh, Berwick and Stirling; later creations were Perth, Dunfermline and Aberdeen. In return for the privilege of exclusive trade within Scotland and *outremare*—overseas—these burghs had to produce dues and taxes on their trade goods; this they did, trading *outremare* in the exports of fish, skins and furs, wool and perhaps a little coal, and importing wine, salt, a little spice, fine linen and tableware, olive oil, marmalade-oranges, hemp and dyestuffs. This pattern, like King David's burghs, expanded but did not change significantly for nearly seven hundred years.

King David coined the first Scots money

Throughout the eleventh and twelfth centuries Scotland was ruled by the line of Malcolmsons, Normanized kings, who did occasional homage to the King of England, and held lands south of the Border like any great English subject. The Pictish lines of the Mormaers were absorbed by Norman knights, who could however only acquire the old native title of earl through marriage to an heiress. Coins, castles, clerics, feudal service, royal burghs and royal sheriffs and justiciars were the chosen instruments of royal power.

King David held, though, to some of the old ways. He had a Celtic bodyguard, of 'durwards', and his army went into battle under the slogan 'Albannaich' (Scots!) and with the full support of the old Celtic earls. This was in the troubled years of the wars between Stephen and Matilda in England. David took this opportunity to assert Scottish independence and though the Scots army was thrown back from Yorkshire, he effectively ruled both Lothian and (briefly) Northumbria, those debatable lands. David's son Henry died before him, and David's designated heir was his grandson Malcolm, who helped the old king govern, and inherited the throne on his death in 1153. David's rule brought Scotland into Europe, as a place of justice, Christian usage and accepted values.

Feudal Scotland emerges

The formal feudal system was adopted gradually and piecemeal, with less enthusiasm by those who already had held the land for generations than by the Norman incomers. Gradually the king ruled as the apex of a feudal system, under

King David and his grandson Malcolm

which he allocated lands to great men who swore by doing homage to do his service. They in turn had vassal lairds with smaller landholdings, and all who held land had the obligation to find knights and men at arms for the royal armies. The peasantry, as they always had done, fought when they had to, and farmed for their livelihood, in a complicated social pattern of freeman, bond and serf.

Great woodlands covered much territory. Many of the forests were hunting grounds and royal preserves. Tiny towns grew up at river crossings and good harbours such as Ayr, Dundee, Aberdeen and Inverness. The king established royal centres of power—wooden castles of a sort—moved round his kingdom consuming the taxes (which were paid in kind) and dispensing justice. The great men, the earls, did the same in their lands. In southern Scotland the Angles who spoke Inglis called their districts shires and the local royal tax gatherer was the shire reeve, a humble bureaucrat. The first shire reeve or sheriff of the great and continuing line of Scots legal officials who is recorded is 'Cospatric, son of Utred, son of Ulfkil', Sheriff of Roxburgh in about 1100. His name is British, his father had an Anglian name, and his grandfather a Norse one. Cospatric was probably pretty typical of the ethnic mix of the new Scotland.

The feudal system was widespread in Europe by then, and most Scotsmen acquiesced. Not all. Somerled Macgillie-brigte, Lord of Argyll, part Gael, part Norse, challenged the king and sailed up the Clyde. The royal troops under Walter the Steward, with the spiritual support and aid of St Mungo, repulsed the invasion and killed Somerled.

King William came next to the throne, brother of Malcolm, a war-loving, dominating figure. He was never called 'Lion' in his lifetime, but we know him now as William the Lion. He encouraged a train of hopeful young knights who followed him, organizing jousts and tilts, with all the fashionable panoply of high chivalry. He pressed the frontiers of the organized realm further north and west, settling Normans beyond Inverness (the Mowats, Freskins and Bissets) and creating knights' feus through Perthshire and the old Pictish lands of Gowrie, Fife, Angus and the Mearns. His inner kingdom was Central Scotland, bordered by the lands of the earls of the west: Lennox, Menteith, Strathearn; north to Atholl and east to Mar. Beyond these heartlands the country was no less Scotland, but the king's officers had not so much authority, and the king himself in his ceaseless journeys round his realm seldom ventured far north. Lothian was settled Scots territory, and the border was defined, if often disputed, roughly from Carlisle to Berwick. In the Northern Isles the Norse earls ruled subjects of the King of Norway, with a loose Norse confederacy taking in the north-west of Scotland, the Hebrides and the seaways down to the Isle of Man.

But the danger came from the south, from the increasing ambition of the Angevins, kings of England and rulers of much of France. William the Lion made a rash bid to recover lost Northumbria, giving just the chance Henry II of England needed. William's attempt was defeated and harsh terms imposed. William did homage to Henry 'for Scotland and his other land'. Henry II was also conquering Ireland at this time; he was an able and expansionist monarch, who consolidated military gains with good legal administration. His sons were not as able and William recovered somewhat, successfully confronting King Richard—another Lion, the Lion-Heart. However, Lion-Heart's brother, King John Lackland, scored one of his few successes against the King of the Scots. As soon as William the Lion was dead his son Alexander II joined with the English barons who put pressure on King John, forcing him eventually to Runnymede and the sealing of the Magna Carta. However Alexander was not, apparently, deeply interested in the rights of barons, nor in those of the common man. The interplay between England and Scotland at this period was not particularly hostile, more a matter of opportunist seizure of chances, played in terms of dynastic marriages and feudal homage by the closely related royal houses. The

21

William the Lion's tourney

kings of England were preoccupied with wars in their French domains, they wanted a peaceful non-combatant neighbour to the north, and this happy state was maintained until the end of the thirteenth century, when Alexander III was dead and Edward I of England an acquisitive old man.

22

II
Wars of Independence

Nostalgia, and wars in the west

HARKING BACK TO the past has always been a strong Scots characteristic, and sometimes a healthy one. The kings of Scotland occasionally were seized with fits of nostalgia, and one of these occurred towards the end of the Malcolmsons' rule. From Malcolm Ceanmhor and Queen Margaret onwards the opposite tendency had prevailed, to give Scotland a Norman feudal basis, importing the concepts current all over Europe. By the time David I died he was acknowledged to be one of the pattern kings of Christendom. His successors began to re-emphasize their native Scottishness.

The coronation ceremony had very old antecedents, and owed little to the Christian church. It took place at Scone, where the waters of the Tay meet the tide, on a hillock that probably represents an old burial barrow. The king was led to the stone on its summit by his doorward, the Earl of Fife, senior of the old Celtic order of earls, and seated on the stone. Other ceremonies make it clear that the ritual derived from the concept of mystic marriage of ruler and country, which would ensure the fertility of crops and beasts, and was celebrated by the witnesses clashing their shields in acclamation. King David revolted against the 'obsequia', which may have included a horse sacrifice, but Alexander II in 1214 seems to have reverted to much of the old ritual, which included the long recital of genealogies by the royal sennachies or bards (but no horse sacrifices). In its essentials the coronation of the Pictish and Scottish kings at Scone was an enactment of a very primitive Indo-European rite, going back to the earliest common Celtic ancestry.

By the time Alexander III was crowned, as a child of seven, at Scone in 1249, the old Scots and Pictish antecedents were strongly stressed. There was good reason. The feudal changes had been made most thoroughly in the ownership of the fertile lands of the Lothians, Central Scotland and north-east through Strathtay and up the coastline till the other fertile grain-basket of the Moray Firth was reached. Sheriffs in royal castles kept law and order. West and north were the pastoral Celtic cowboys, organized loosely by kinship, or under the protection of a strong leader, in groups that tidy bureaucrats in Edinburgh later began calling clans. Furthermore, the acknowledged rule of the kings of Norway over the

Hebrides, the Orkneys and the Shetlands became diluted by troubles at home (taking the form of turbulent noblemen) and the treaty made between the Scots' King Edgar and King Magnus 'Barelegs' of Norway at the end of the eleventh century became a dead letter. (Magnus Barelegs got his by-name probably because he wore the Highland kilted plaid rather than the Norse trousers.) Thus, during the twelfth century, neither the King of the Scots nor the King of Norway held much authority in the north-west, and the warrior-nobility fought among themselves, feuding for cattle and lands in an untrammelled free-for-all. The Gaelic strain was beginning to predominate in the Hebrides despite the leaders' Norse names; old links with Ireland were re-established, and the Abbey of Iona, decayed and neglected, was revived by Somerled of Argyll, who brought in Irish Benedictine monks from Derry. King William quite rightly considered this politically unacceptable, and quickly installed some very conventional mainland Benedictines there. For one thing the English under Henry II were engaged in an early attempt to subdue Ireland, and the King of the Scots did not want to be mixed up in that affair, nor to emphasise kinship with the Irish.

It became urgent to settle the mainland of Scotland, and in particular to curb the pretentions of those local chiefs in the west. The Lord of the Isles must not encroach too far on the mainland. So the kings of the Scots began to re-emphasise their own Scots and Pictish roots. Bards and sennachies began to reappear at the royal court, singing of ancestral deeds, and Norman knights and clerics found it prudent to learn the Gaelic tongue, which had spread widely among ordinary folk, even into the Lothians and Galloway.

Meantime the grip of the kings of Norway slackened over the Hebrides, but was still firm over Orkney and Shetland. In the Isle of Man the Norse kings still collected taxes but the lords of Man used their key position to play off England, Ireland and Scotland as it suited those seafaring descendants of Norse pirates. Somerled of Argyll, as we have seen, made a bid for the lands of the Clyde and was defeated by Walter the Steward with the ghostly aid of St Mungo. Walter the Steward was personally the gainer by his victory over Somerled, and the Stewarts, or Stuarts, acquired Bute and later Cowal and much else in the south-west Highlands. At Rothesay, in Bute, the Steward built the first stone castle of a

Norman pattern in the west of Scotland, a great circular keep guarding the safe anchorage of Rothesay Bay. His example was soon followed, and stone castles rose frowning over all the anchorages of the west. Castle Sween, Kisimul in Barra, Dunstaffnage in Lorne, Duart in Mull, Mingary, Tioram, Ardtornish in Morven, and Skipness, are only a few battered survivors of a sudden surge of baronial power expressed in classic thirteenth-century style, in stone curtain walls and square keeps.

King William the Lion was not so interested in his Highland problems as his two successors were. Alexander II, perhaps as a result of his hark-back to ancestral ways, took to boats again, and discovered the old truth that to rule the west it was necessary to be mobile, to have a navy. Northern boatbuilders had a good reputation; the Count of St Pol in Normandy sent to Inverness to have a great ship built there, to go on crusade in 1248. Alexander effectively patrolled western waters, but only for a short time before his death. All the lords of the west had vessels too, birlins—small craft to sail or row—which they carved on their tombstones and bore on their coats of arms, as some still do. The lords of Galloway, Man and Ulster attempted to gang up, and even to indicate delicately that a little English support (against Alexander II) would not be amiss. Round about 1220 Alexander succeeded in defeating this, and depressed the pretentions of, among others, Duncan Lord of Carrick, whose great-grandson was King Robert the Bruce.

Another name also comes to the fore now. In Alexander's successful campaign in Galloway he put the captured rebels in charge of a trusty Norman knight, John de Balliol, who then married the remaining heiress of Galloway and thus (by Pictish succession through his wife, Devorgilla) became the Lord of Galloway, and a loyal king's liege. The inheritance of the lords of Carrick passed by marriage to a Norman from Bruis in the Cotenin.

The penetration of the west was not wholly by the sword. All these great lords were pious sons of the church, endowing churches and monasteries: Somerled or his son Reginald endowed the first medieval monastery in the west, at Saddell in Kintyre, before 1134. Soon many other monasteries were endowed, small houses but in touch with great European mother houses. Norsemen, about this time, were stormbound in Orkney on their way to a crusade in Jerusalem, and sheltered in the great chambered cairn of Maes Howe, 4000 years old, strongly built and secure. They left

Rothesay Castle

their graffiti on its walls. A barefoot cleric from Argyll also went off on crusade, as many others did, and some Gaelic fragments of his verse survive:

Help from Cruachan is far off across the wave-bordered Mediterranean,
The journeying of spring separates us
From these green-branched glens . . .

Muiredhach Albanach

One of the more stalwart members of clan Campbell, Colin of Glenorchy, got the by-name 'Black Colin of Rome' and fought at Rhodes against the Turk. There were plenty of Scots in the mainstream of European life.

The history of the Macdougalls of Lorne is characteristic of the times. Dougal, son of the defeated Somerled, established a wide personal lordship in Argyll and saw advantage in making his peace with the King of Scotland. His younger brother, however, took a more traditional view and went plundering off by ship to Ireland, where he achieved a right-and-left by slaying an English sheriff and marrying his daughter to the King of Connaught. Dougal's sons, however, became loyal lieges of the King of Scotland.

When Alexander III took control of the kingdom at the age of 20 he at once showed determination to oust the remaining Norsemen from possession. The west was garrisoned and the oak woods rang with axes as a new fleet was built. Old King Haakon of Norway sailed with his dragon-headed fleet to defend his Scottish realms. The lords of the Isles and the mainland were hard put to see whom to support to their own advantage. Macdougall of Lorne stood firm to his new lord, the King of Scotland; Macdonald of Islay and MacSween tried to sit on the fence, so that Haakon took hostages from them before forcing them out in his following. In the Clyde in early October 1263 a sea skirmish was followed by the land battle of Largs, with King Haakon himself coming ashore, and battle axes flashing. In the end of the day the Norsemen retreated, back eventually to Orkney where Haakon died. The old Norse empire had crumbled, the men of the Isles had become from Haakon's point of view undependable, more Gaels than Norse. Only the Northern Isles remained. In the treaty of Perth of 1266 that followed, the Scots paid the Norsemen an indemnity, and took the Western Isles. Later King Alexander's only daughter Margaret was handfasted to King Eric of Norway; this was a popular royal wedding in 1281. Fighting the Northmen ceased, trading across the North Sea strengthened, and the King of Scots quietly consolidated the royal hold of mainland Scotland, and established rights over the Hebrides. King Magnus kept the Northern Isles.

Alexander III's reign lasted 40 years, and people grew to look back on it as one of Scotland's golden ages. His wife and children all died before him, and at the end of his life he took a new young wife, to get new heirs. He rode back to her at Kinghorn, from Edinburgh, crossing to Fife by the Queen's Ferry one stormy night in 1286 with nobles in the castle and burgesses on the ferry plucking at his sleeve, trying to dissuade him from so rash a journey. They were right—he rode his horse over a cliff in the dark and was killed. The realm of Scotland mourned him:

> Quhen Alexander our Kynge was dede
> That Scotland lede in lauch and le,
> Away was sons of alle and bredd
> Off Wyne and wax, of gamyn and gle.
> Our golde was changit into lede.
> Christ, born in virgynyte
> Succour Scotland and remede
> That is stade in perplexite.[1]

> (Anon)

'Quhen Alexander our Kynge was dede'

The consequence of Alexander III's death was the long dispute for the throne of Scotland that ended when the Bruce had consolidated his hold. But that was after many years and wars of independence. The storm clouds did not break as soon as the king was dead. His heir was hardly three years old, his only granddaughter Margaret the Maid of Norway. It was one of the many points when the old tanist rules of succession would have perhaps provided a ruler who was legitimate, adult and male—three most desirable requirements for a thirteenth-century monarch. The Scotsmen of the day did well, under the circumstances. Guardians of the Realm were appointed, a nicely balanced council of six men, clergy and nobles, who ruled in the name of the Community of Scotland, and who struck a new seal with St Andrew on his cross and the appeal 'Andrew Be leader of the Scots, your fellow countrymen!' Out of the tangled bloodlines of Picts, Scots, Angles, Welshmen, Northmen, Normans and Flemings, the community of Scotland was emerging, with as clear a national identity as any

[1] When Alexander our King was dead
That led Scotland in law and peace, away
Was all abundance of ale and bread,
Candlelit parties, wine and fun—
Our gold was changed into lead.
Christ, born in virginity
Succour Scotland and remedy
Us who stand in perplexity.

King Alexander fell to his death

other nation-state of the Middle Ages. There was not even a common language; court documents cite the inhabitants of Scotland as 'Scottis, Erse, French and Gallovigian', and some add in the Flemings in the trading burghs. For all that, there was a cohesion and a sense of identity that was tough enough to stand the hammer blows of the English when they came.

They came by invitation. Edward Plantagenet was the great-uncle of the Maid of Norway, her grandmother was his sister. And Edward was about the most puissant prince in Europe in the late thirteenth century. The Guardians asked his advice, both as king and as a close kinsman of the child queen. They made an agreement to betroth her to the child Edward Prince of Wales, eldest son of King Edward, and they sent for her to come from Norway: 'To Norroway, to Norroway, to Norroway over the foam, the King's daughter from Norroway, 'tis thou must bring her home.' There is no trace of Sir Patrick Spens in the historic record but the ballad carries the feel of urgent political decisions, bad weather, and royal journeys ending in disaster. The actual disaster was the death of the child queen after her arrival in Orkney; she died in the arms of the Bishop of Bergen. She was nine years old. At least she was saved a disastrous marriage to Edward Prince of Wales, who was, it later turned out, homosexual. With her died the old blood line of the kings of Scotland, from Kenneth mac Alpin onwards. At once, like a crop of dragon's teeth, the Claimants sprang up, and the Guardians of the Realm lost their hold.

The Claimants

There were 14 Claimants whose claims were good enough to be considered, many others whose claims were laughable. Edward, who had peace in his French domains and who had imposed his rule on the principality of Wales, was ready to assert his rights over Scotland. Two hundred years before, Malcolm Ceanmhor had become the vassal of William, and subsequent kings of Scotland had sworn fealty for lands held of the King of England. The lawyers of the day in England declared the Scots to be the vassals of England, the Scots lawyers were equally adamant that homage had only been done on a personal level, and for English lands, not for the realm of Scotland. Since the days of the early Malcolmsons, the King of Scots had also been Lord of the Honour of Huntingdon, for which each had sworn fealty to the King of England. The invitation to arbitrate in the affairs of Scotland came to Edward I at a significant moment: his wife Eleanor had just died, his other lands were fairly settled and his efficient lawyers were busily erecting a complicated structure of administration from Aquitaine to Carlisle and Caernarvon. Why not press the Scottish claim and unify the whole island? Edward moved cautiously, though he behaved later with great violence; he began within legal limits, meeting the Scots Guardians and a gathering of other great men at Norham on the Tweed, and putting on them the onus of proving that Scotland was *not* a vassal of state of England. He also let fall that the Scots might have to prove their independence by the sword. After three weeks a divided council of Scots agreed to recognize him as overlord, but they always denied his right to parcel up the realm of Scotland like any baronial holding, and to divide it up amongst his adherents. By June 1291 Edward's men held the royal castles and centres of authority in Scotland.

The difficulty in deciding a succession lay in the comparatively small families that generations of the royal house of Malcolm had had, making the choice narrow and based on far-back marriages and births. Part of Alexander III's skill in governing lay in his wide distribution of offices of the crown, so that by his death the majority of the earls and bishops and many of the barons of the realm had some experience of holding office. From these competent ranks were drawn 80 Scots auditors to hear the claims, as were the claimants also: the magnates of Scotland had married into royal circles. But before the claims could be heard, Edward of England harried the Scots into conceding that he was overlord of the realm of Scotland; great numbers of them swore allegiance to him, in a green field on the English bank of the Tweed.

The court constituted was large, a jury of 105 men considered the claims as 25 English auditors were added. Of the 14 claims, ten were put in for reasons of prestige, and four were based on legitimate descent from Henry Earl of Northumberland, who died before his father King David, in 1152, and his son Earl David. The four were Balliol, Bruce, Hastings of Abergavenny and Florent Count of Holland. The Count of Holland produced a dubious story that King William the Lion had designated his great-great-grandmother Ada as his heir, and wasted a lot of the court's time in a vain search for supporting papers to prove it.

Hastings simply claimed that Scotland was not a kingdom, merely a demesne or royal estate, which (unlike a kingdom) could be divided amongst the heirs. His lawyers modestly only requested a share of the realm for Hastings, but his claim was eventually dismissed out of hand.

This left Balliol and Bruce. Balliol was the grandson of Earl David's eldest daughter, and claimed through primogeniture, which was only just becoming generally accepted in Scotland. Bruce was the son of Earl David's second daughter, so stood a generation nearer to royal blood, and this carried weight under the half-forgotten earlier customs. After much patient debate the auditors chose Balliol, a fair decision in a difficult case.

Balliol was enthroned at Scone with traditional ritual, and Edward immediately made it clear that though he tolerated these customs, he retained his overlordship. John Balliol had to swear fealty many times over, and to do homage for his kingdom to the King of England. Edward treated him with scant courtesy. Balliol soon had to produce Scots troops for Edward's war in France, where his subjects in Gascony had risen in arms. The Scots revolted, and were easily overcome by an English army at Dunbar, as classic a site as Twickenham for a regular encounter. Balliol was an ineffective king, one whom a chronicler described kindly as 'a lamb among wolves'. He was forced to abdicate.

Edward made a royal progress north-east, following the route Agricola had taken 1200 years before, and scorching the earth. Even the apple orchards were cut down by the English army. Edward took the Coronation Stone of Destiny with him from Scone to Westminster Abbey, where it remains. The royal castles were all garrisoned by English troops, the sheriffs were all of Edward's appointment. Most of the nobles of Scotland suffered from divided allegiance. Many also held English lands, reflecting in miniature the original dilemma of the kings of Scotland. Most thought it prudent to agree with the mighty Edward and hold on to their lands. Many retreated to their own strongholds and kept low.

Wallace and Bruce

When revolt again came it was not led by a great noble, but by the younger son of a Lanarkshire bonnet-laird, William Wallace, and his friend Andrew Moray, kin of the Norman family of Freskin de Moravia who had adapted their name to their great holdings on the Moray Firth. Wallace and Moray appealed to the 'middling sort' in Scotland, who flocked to their standard. Acting in the name of King John Balliol and the Guardians of the Realm of Scotland they mustered and trained a small guerilla force, and won a brilliant battle at Stirling Bridge. The English garrison emerged from the castle, over the only bridge across the Forth and along a perilous narrow causeway. Moray and Wallace lay hidden in thick woods and pounced out on the heavily armed English, driving the wounded to drown in the surrounding marsh. It was a rude shock to the English army, guerilla tactics had little place in the current rules of formal warfare. It was also a galvanic shock to Scotland, hope was rekindled. Andrew Moray died of wounds and at Falkirk, without him, Wallace was defeated in a conventional battle, and went into years of hiding, ending in ultimate arrest and execution. Skirmishes and English retaliations rumbled on, Balliol was in France and the barons of Scotland were each petty rulers of their domains, under England. It was not for some years after the Battle of Stirling that Edward of England felt secure.

In 1305 one of these barons came forward with a new claim; he was Robert Bruce, lord of Carrick and Annandale, grandson of the Claimant in 1291, after the Maid of Norway's death. The first object of Bruce was to unite support behind him. He was already a rebel in Edward's eyes, and a desperate man.

He acted with support from many nobles, including those of the house of Comyn—one of the most influential families in Scotland. Comyns had been adjudicators and servants of the crown for three generations, and they held great lands in the north-east and near Glasgow. Bruce and John, the Red Comyn, cooperated in the campaigns waged sporadically against the English occupying

army. The head of the clan was the Earl of Buchan, and there were many other active members of the Comyn connection. Bruce and John Comyn, with the Bishop of St Andrews, were Guardians of the Realm in the exile of John Balliol, and strong opponents of the English. When by 1305 the English armies had prevailed, Comyn and Bruce were among those who made their peace with Edward. They soon were making a secret pact that Comyn would help Bruce towards the crown, and be rewarded with land. The events will never be known in detail, but Bruce met Comyn in the abbey church of Dumfries; they talked, quarrelled, and Bruce stabbed the Red Comyn to death at the high altar steps.

Although this rather naturally alienated the large Comyn family, enough of the magnates of Scotland and bishops of the church rallied to Bruce to make a hasty coronation possible. There was a King of the Scots again, a rallying point. Bruce then lost a battle at Methven, and had to go into hiding to escape Edward's wrath; his family were imprisoned and treated with savagery, and his prospects seemed poor. He emerged from a retreat in the Western Isles, and conducted long, brilliantly successful, hit-and-run campaigns against the hated garrison castles of Edward.

Bannockburn and after

Finally, by 1313, only Stirling Castle remained in English hands, held for Edward II by Sir Philip de Moubray, with whom Bruce's brother Edward made a deal. The siege would be called off for the winter months, and the truce would last until midsummer day, on which day Stirling Castle would be surrendered if it had not been relieved by England. Edward I had died in 1307 and it was for Edward II that the garrison watched. It was a long watch, it was only on the eve of midsummer 1314 that the pennants and standards of England could be seen as the army marched along the firm old Roman military road behind the Antonine Wall. Edward had brought a huge force, with a host of flamboyant knights, heroes of the joust and tiltyard, whom he couldn't control very well. His inexperience allowed Bruce to choose the meeting ground, on the boggy banks of the Bannock Burn. In a hard long battle the small peasant army of Bruce, led by the lairds of Scotland, defeated the flower of chivalry. The King of England was hustled away, hotly pursued by Douglas, and Moubray came out of Stirling Castle and did homage to Bruce. A number of English lords were taken prisoner, and held to ransom by the Scots.

Bannockburn was a tactical victory and a national triumph: it was by no means the end of English intervention, nor the end of factions amongst the Scots leaders. Bruce's support was still only partial. It has been described as 'Celtic', but he had to wage civil war against such old families as the Macnabs in Central Perthshire and the MacDougalls of Lorne, as well as the Comyn clan in Buchan. Families of Norman and Norse origin fought in his armies.

The Scots alliance with France, which became sentimentally known as 'the

Bruce killed de Bohun before Bannockburn

auld alliance', developed during the wars of independence, mainly because France saw advantage in intermittent support of England's enemy, as they themselves were often at war with England. The Scots always thought more of the alliance than the French, who were fair-weather friends.

Bruce's most telling support came from the Scottish church, who saw in an independent King of Scots their surest shield against the Pope's threatened absorption of the Scots church into the English See of York. They carried the holiest relic of St Columba in Scotland, the Brecbannach, into battle at Bannockburn. A skilful propaganda war was simultaneously waged by the clerics, Edward's camp making much of Bruce's excommunication for Comyn's murder in a church, and his unlawful seizure of the throne. The Scots prelates fought back, claiming correctly that the Scots' conversion to Christ was earlier than the English; perhaps, they further claimed, by St Andrew himself. Edward's chancery put forward the equally mythical story of King Brutus the Trojan, Edward's 'ancestor', who united the whole island in the unimaginably dim past. The Scots clerics won this war by composing the incomparable Latin Declaration

35

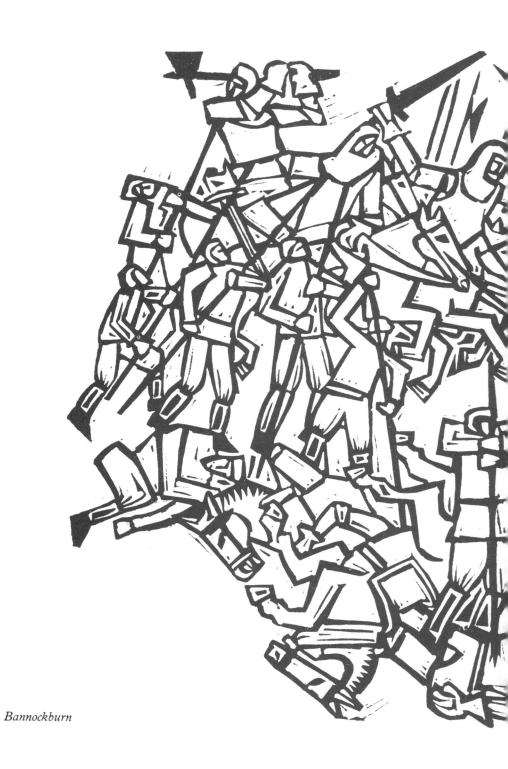

Bannockburn

of Arbroath in the name of the nobles of Scotland, addressed to the Pope. In 1320 John XXII, the dithering old holder of the See of Rome, gave way and acknowledged the right of Bruce to the throne, and the ringing claim of Scots: 'So long as a hundred of us remain alive we will never be subject to the English, since it is not for riches, honours or glory that we fight, but for liberty alone, which no worthy man loses save with his life.'

This long round of the War of Independence was concluded at the Treaty of Northampton in 1328. Edward had lost his father's ambitions, in 1327 he lost his throne to his son. Bruce was old and dying. His child son David II was then crowned, and challenged by Balliol's son. In the 1330s another short round of the Independence struggle took place. David II later rashly took an invading army into Durham, where he was taken prisoner by the English, who kept him 11 years. For the next 200 years the war between Scotland and England was endemic, each generation challenging 'the auld enemy', but the independence of the kingdom of Scotland was no longer questioned. Dissatisfied Scots nobles went over the border to enlist English help, English pretenders to the crown of England turned up hopefully at the court of the King of Scots. The Percys sought help north of the border. It was a fluid, fighting period, and rather inconclusive.

Country mice and town mice

Under these high and largely ineffectual skirmishings the folk of Scotland went on in their accustomed way. 'Mart' beasts were slain and salted at Martinmas in the autumn, a few thin cattle survived the winter on a precarious diet of chopped whin, sharing the smoky family hearth. Bere barley, milk and cheese provided a basic diet, plain but reasonably nourishing. The little fields were run-rigged in big banked strips, each ferm-toun dividing the good and bad lands amongst the able-bodied. There was plenty of grumbling about taxes, customs dues, military

service, food shortage or famine, epidemics (which raged unchecked), the demands of the church for Peter's Pence, and the great standby, the Scottish weather. Even court poets sang their complaints about that.

> In to thir dirk and drublie dayis
> Quhone sabill all the hevin arrayis
> With mystie vapouris, cluddis, and skyis,
> Nature all curage me denyis . . .[2]
>
> William Dunbar

But there were the great fairs to look forward to, twice a year under royal licence up and down the country from Caithness to the border, and weekly markets in the small burghs, where little ships slipped into harbour from the Baltic or the Low Countries. Pilgrimages were also diversions, usually to local and minor shrines. The healing wells had been sacred long before Christ, and kept their repute, particularly for the complaints that were intractable to herbal cures; the mad and barren and blind were taken to wells. And the great pagan feasts of Beltane and Lammas (May 1 and August 1) were kept, along with Yule, Easter and Hallows, with such regularity that farm accounts to the middle of the eighteenth century still used Beltane to date their rent days. A vivid glimpse of the contrasts developing between the town and the country is given in the long version of an Aesop's fable written by Henryson, schoolmaster of Dunfermline in the late Middle Ages:

> [2] Into the dark and dismal days
> When sable all the heavens arrays
> With misty vapour, clouds, and skies,
> Nature all courage me denies . . .

The Taill of the Uponlandis Mous and the Burges Mous

This rurall mous into the wynter-tyde
Had hunger, cauld, and tholit grit distress
The uther mous that in the burgh can byde
Was gild-brother and made an fre burges—
Toll-fre als, but custum mair or les,
And fredome had to ga quhairver scho list,
Among the cheis in ark, and meill in kist.[3]

The scattered monasteries gave some refuge to the old or leprous, 'Spittal Streets' in many towns still witness that there were hospitals of a sort, as Cressid's father found when his daugther was stricken, in another poem of Henryson's. Education

[3] *The Tale of the Country Mouse and Town Mouse*

This rural mouse had through the winter time
Hunger and cold, and suffered great distress:
The other mouse, that in the town did live
Was a guild-brother and made a free burgess—
Toll-free, that is, she paid Customs more or less,
And had freedom to go wherever she chose
Among the cheese in cupboards or the meal in chests.

A good herbal remedy for hangovers was found among the papers of a Burgess of Aberdeen

41

King James 1

was patchy and mainly in the hands of churchmen, and regarded as preliminary to a career in the church. The burghs and cathedral towns mostly employed a schoolmaster. The Scots were not a rich nation, but they found the money to endow Glasgow and St Andrews universities in the fifteenth century, and later Aberdeen with two. The Friars came to Scotland and preached to the poor, later they became known for their libraries and learning. The great prelates rebuilt the cathedrals, the high kirks of St Giles in Edinburgh, St Johnstoun of Perth, and Holy Rude in Stirling, and the royal court continued to rely on the ability of prelates to run the court and chancery, and to conduct foreign relations and go on embassy.

Royal inheritance

The confusion of the royal inheritance was settled in an unexpected way. Bruce's only daughter had married one of his greatest supporters, Walter the Steward, Lord of Bute and much else. Their son Robert II succeeded his uncle David II on the throne of Scotland in 1371, and Robert III followed him in 1390. Neither were strong kings, and Edward Balliol remained a legitimate alternative. The dubious legitimacy of the line was forgotten under habit, though when the Stewart James I came to the throne (after his elder brother the Duke of Rothesay had come to a mysterious end) it would have been a fine prophet who foretold a further 250 years' unbroken Stewart (or Stuart) succession. None apparently was so rash. There were a number of great nobles, royal kin—such as the royal earls of Ross, and the great house of Black Douglas, the earls of Strathearn and Menteith and the house of Atholl—who each held their head very high, and had such a good conceit of their birth that the sons of the palace steward often had to fight for their title as King of the Scots. Moreover four Stewarts inherited the crown as infants, and there were seven minorities in ten reigns.

James I learned the craft of kingship the hard way; when he was finishing his education he went to fight in the army of the King of France as a necessary part of a chivalric training. Unfortunately the English took James prisoner on his way to France. He remained in English hands all his youth, for 17 years, as his uncle Earl of Albany, Regent of Scotland, saw absolutely no compelling reason to wring out the large ransom demanded of the Scots, nor to give up his own profitable farming of the revenues of Scotland. Such meetings of Parliament as had been held now ceased, the income of the lands and burghs of Scotland was appropriated by various nobles; it was the rule of the big bad barons, administered by sword and quieter dirk. Eventually James returned; he promised to raise his own ransom and the English were rather bored with the bother and expense of keeping a royal prisoner so long. James had picked up a good education in these long years, and had fallen in love with Joan de Beaufort, whom he brought north as queen. He wrote her fashionably sentimental love poems in his long imprisonment:

The Field of Thistles

A! swete, ar ye a warldly creature
Or hevinly thing in likness of nature
Or ar ye god cupidis owin princesse
And cummyn ar to lous me of band?[1]

James I comes into his own

He acted decisively on his return. His aged and plausible uncle Albany had died so he executed his red-headed cousin Murdo, the regent's son, and others of his kin, on the hanging hill outside Stirling Castle. He disposed of some of the other trouble-makers by sending Atholl and Strathearn to England as hostages for his

ransom. This unfortunately only strengthened the claims of the more distant royal kin, the earls of Ross, who gave future trouble. James intended to rule through a parliament, he had observed the English and French models. A shadowy Scots Parliament had existed since the Alexanders had extended their council with larger periodic gatherings, but that was long in the past. James's Parliaments were the first to include representatives of the royal burghs, as the wealth of the kingdom was in the towns as well as in the wide lands. Parliament's two main duties were to revise the laws, and to raise the revenue; even in the fifteenth century lawgiving and fund raising needed some measure of consent from the people. James I's stated object was 'That the key would keep the castle and the bracken bush the Kye', by which he implied that the poor man's cattle could graze safely and the baron's depredations would be curbed. James's Parliaments at his behest passed a lot of statutes, some excellent, some unenforceable. It was one thing to state the equality of all men before the law, but quite another to try to ban totally the playing of football so that men could practise archery. James II put an equally ineffective ban on golf for the same object, but the Scots continued to play football and golf, and to be poor archers.

[1] Ah, sweet, are you a worldly creature
Or heavenly thing in the likeness of nature
Or are you god Cupid's own princess
And come to loose my prison bonds?

Though the burghs were growing, and overseas trade in Scots fish and rather rough woollen goods increased, there was little actual cash about, and all the great estates were paid their dues mainly in natural produce. This meant that the castle yards were full of scrawny hens paid as Cain rent, and that varieties of chicken broth, from cock-a-leekie to queen of soups ('tak six hens . . .') became the culinary delight of the Scot's kitchen. Cash rents, called 'silver mail', formed a smaller proportion of the whole, and were often only exacted from distant properties, due to the difficulty of bringing in heavy or perishable produce to the collecting point. The kings of Scotland, and their nobles, began building castles—fortified, but with halls, solars and bedchambers which offered some

comfort. The capital of Scotland was where the king and the court were, and this might be Edinburgh, Stirling, Perth or Linlithgow, or the lesser castles of the realm. The court moved throughout the year, taking with it carts of 'plenishings', the charter-chests, the tapestries, the window-glass, the great beds and coffers, and the real live Lion of Scotland in a heavy caged cart. After a month or two in each palace the local produce brought in as Cain rent would have been eaten up and the stench from the dirty straw on the floors and from the privies would have become too strong, so the court moved on, leaving the seneschal to clean up and to take in more rents of barley, cheese, hens, mutton and honey, and to replenish the peat stacks.

It was in Perth that James I died in 1437, stabbed in his lodging by a conspiracy of Atholl men and Grahams resentful of royal control. But they failed to win popular support, and the infant heir was not killed. James II began his rule as a minor, but accepted as king. His problem as he grew up was the increase in power again of the lords of his realm. The Livingstone connection did exceedingly well, dominating his early days. He managed to be rid of them once he was married to Mary of Gueldres at the age of 18, only to have much worse trouble with the Black Douglas family. The Douglas held vast tracts of southern Scotland, from coast to coast, and dominated the political scene by sheer defiance and strength. Of all the barons in Scotland, Douglas was the most independent. The king asked Douglas to dinner in Stirling Castle, they quarrelled and James stabbed him to death. The Douglas's cronies, Crawford and Malise Graham, with distant backing from the Lord of the Isles, challenged the king and burnt the town of Stirling, but Parliament endorsed the king and he built up support by gifts of land to other nobles.

James was a modern man, and developed a passion for gunnery. This was so expensive, so newfangled, that only the king owned any artillery. The great stronghold castles of his barons became vulnerable to royal attack, and when the last of the Black Douglas clan fortified their castles the king advanced slowly with his trundling guns, at three miles a day, and blew them up at leisure. Predictably his enthusiasm went too far, and James II was killed by the explosion of a gun at the siege of Roxburgh, during an English invasion, in 1460.

Another minority

Another pleasurable minority lay ahead of the Scots nobles, as James III was only a boy. At once the sole remaining Douglas, in exile in the Yorkist camp in England, engineered a treaty against the king with the Lord of the Isles and the English. This was signed secretly at Ardtornish Castle, one of the MacDonald strongholds in the west. News of the projected carve-up, between England, the MacDonald and the Douglas only leaked out some years after; the English were too occupied with the Wars of the Roses at the time to take full advantage.

King James II

King James III

III

Renaissance Scotland

James III

JAMES III in many ways was a typical Stewart, with a long, ugly and intelligent face. He foreshadowed the policy of later kings of his line with the new emphasis he placed on the prestige of the monarchy. James III had imperial dreams. This led him to be autocratic with his nobles, who since his father had cast down the power of the Black Douglas lacked a dominating leader. (The Red Douglas family had not yet risen to power.) In James III's time a new pattern developed, the houses of Argyll and Huntly began their rise to territorial and political power. The court adopted greater display and formality, to impress both nobles and visiting foreigners with the puissance of the king.

James, however, was without the personal charm that so many of his line possessed, nor did he travel so widely as many kings did in the realm, to know and be known by his people. He ruled, as his predecessors had done, through the King-in-Parliament. This body was assembled nearly every year and offered an opportunity for influential men to put forward grievances and to endorse and discuss the laws the king put before them. The Scotsmen in Parliament were not the equivalent of the English shire gentry but were drawn from the dominant nobility, the Lords in Parliament, together with representatives of the higher clergy and of the royal burghs: Sir David Lindsay later wrote *Ane Satire of the Thrie Estaitis* based on the system of representation. The business of the crown was almost entirely conducted by churchmen, the only men trained in the law and in administration. Again unlike the English system, taxation was only levied for special emergencies (most often a war with England), and was generally not heavy. Rents for crown lands provided most of the small revenue. Justice was largely a matter for local dispensation, with burgh courts or baron courts handling most disputes. There was no police force and even the sheriffs had few enforcement officers.

James III was unpopular. The nobility distrusted his passion for building halls and palaces and derided his inability to sit well on horseback. Far more serious, however, were the corroding suspicions created by his autocratic personal style of ruling. He doubted the loyalty of his nobles, whom he treated arbitrarily to suit his own acquisitive ends, and they in turn suspected him. In the end some revolted, first in an obscure threatening foray against James at Lauder, and finally in an ambush at Sauchieburn where he was killed. He had ruled for 20 years.

The lordship of the Isles

Successive kings of Scots faced the problem that the Islands were an independent princedom, along with large mainland areas of the north-west. Seagoing ships gave to the Hebrides and the sea lochs of the mainland a much greater unity than they have today; the long rule of the Norsemen gave a cultural unity also. In Gaelic tradition the first Lord of the Isles was Somerled, in the twelfth century; it has recently been shown that an ancestor of his, Godfrey son of Fergus, was so described as far back as the ninth century. However, Norse rule for nearly three hundred years intervened between Godfrey and Somerled, and Somerled remains the best starting point for an inquiry into the lordship of the Isles. He married into the ruling Norse family of the Isle of Man and moved into occupation of some of mainland Argyll. Halting him on the Clyde proved decisive for the fortunes of Walter the Steward, progenitor of the Stewart line.

Somerled's son and two grandsons gave their names to their clans. The lands they owned were wide. Clan Dougal were on Mull and mainland Lorn, clan Donald lived from Kintyre to Islay and Morven, and clan Ruari on the Uists and the mainland from Moidart to Knoydart. Skye and the Lewis remained possessions of the King of Man until in 1266 these lands were ceded by Norway to Scotland and were disputed by MacDonalds and MacLeods. The Scottish wars of independence brought these distant clans into the national arena. Clan Dougal sided with Balliol, and was attacked by Bruce, and later lost some lands. Clan Donald and clan Ruari gave Bruce aid and comfort, and were later rewarded.

The lords of the Isles and the earls of Ross

By the mid-fourteenth century clan Donald predominated, absorbing the branch of Ruari through marriage, and thus dominating a huge area of the west. From 1350 onward four MacDonald lords followed in direct succession: John of Islay, Donald, Alexander and John. These used the formal title (in Latin) of Lord of the Isles. John of Islay married a royal bride, a daughter of Robert Stewart, later King Robert II. From King Robert also were descended the earls of Ross, whose lands centred on Dingwall, the old border town between the Norse of Caithness and Sutherland and the Mormaer of Moray's possessions. Easter Ross was fertile and populous.

Relations between the lords of the Isles and the earls of Ross fluctuated, after a battle the peace was usually sealed with a marriage contract. They came to a crisis in 1411 at the bloody and indecisive battle of Harlaw. The Regent Albany, enjoying unfettered expansion for the family of the earls of Buchan during the imprisonment of his nephew James I, appeared to be on the point of swallowing up the earldom of Ross. At this time the lordship of Ross was held by the countess, a young niece of the wife of the Lord of the Isles. It is not clear whether the Lord of the Isles marched his men to Aberdeenshire to protect her by attacking the Regent Albany's faction, or to make himself King of the Scots. The Lord of the Isles was forced to withdraw, and made his peace with James I on his return from captivity. He gave hostages for good behaviour. James I as part of his campaign to curb his lawless nobles later marched north in 1429, and eventually took prisoner Alexander, the next Lord of the Isles, who was particularly pugnacious. Alexander also gave security for good behaviour. He was released and made Earl of Ross and lived on the mainland, turning his back on the Isles. Although there is little evidence, what there is tends to show that he had not a very strong grip over Easter Ross; he was, however, buried there, in Fortrose, in 1449.

The Secret Treaty of Ardtornish

Alexander's son John returned to the Isles, where he became a clandestine ally of the Douglas faction in southern Scotland, and with Edward of York. The Secret Treaty of Ardtornish followed in 1461 while James III was still young, in which the Lord of the Isles, Douglas, and Edward of York pledged each other to divide up Scotland between them. It came to nothing. John continued to act as a prince, Lord of the Isles and Earl of Ross. After nine years the Secret Treaty's provisions became known, and John's lands were forfeited. Most were returned, except Ross, on royal conditions and narrow terms, and the king rebuilt a strong royal castle at a forward position at Tarbert Loch Fyne. Eventually in 1494, after further feuding and lawlessness, the lands of the Lord of the Isles were finally forfeited and John became a royal prisoner for the last ten years of his life. The lordship remained in the king's hands, and Ross became an extinct title. There were, however, constant risings and revolts in the old lordship for at least fifty years more, and the lost lordship contributed to the inherent instability of the area long after that.

Scots abroad

From James III's day in the late 1400s little dramatic happened in Scottish history until the great upheaval of the Reformation more than a century later, except for the short disastrous war which ended at Flodden Field. This long, fallow period was unusual amongst contemporary European nations, and in its slow course Scotland matured. James I's old ideal of the kye in the bracken and the keys of the castles in royal hands was, by and large, realized. And the Scots early developed their taste for seeking fortune overseas. The four universities which were founded offered courses much like sixth-form colleges today, and took their students young, in their early teens. The able then went to Leyden or Paris, to Bologna or Rome, to complete their studies. Scotland produced some international Latin scholars: Duns Scotus the Dominican, in the thirteenth century, later Hector Boece and John Major, and, later still George Buchanan. Her merchants traded with France and the Low Countries, and after some trials the Convention of Royal Burghs established a staple port at Campvere on the Island of Walcheren where the quays are still paved with good Aberdeen granite setts, the export of a poor country sent over as ballast.

Then, and for hundreds of years later, soldiering provided the easiest passport overseas; the nobility sent their sons to the petty courts of Europe to learn manners and military drills, while poorer men sold their swords to foreign armies. Scots were more familiar with France, Sweden, the German states and Italy than with England, where few were tempted to venture to a chilly welcome as merchants or soldiers; nor did they go to England for education. In the Baltic states of the Hanseatic League Scots dealers early settled, selling herrings for the Friday fasts of Catholic Europe. So successful were they that salt herring became exempt, by Papal decree, from the ban on eating flesh on days of abstinence, and passed into a proverb defining the indefinable: 'Neither fish, flesh nor gude red herring'.

James III, in his wayward fashion, had dabbled in foreign affairs. His own marriage was a dynastic triumph; he married Margaret of Denmark and Norway in 1468, and the impoverished Northmen of the day put Orkney and Shetland into pawn to raise the royal dowry. The pledges have never been redeemed, and the Scots have considered the Northern Isles an integral part of Scotland since that day. The Northern Islanders, however, sometimes still dream of a return to a Norse hegemony. James III attempted a sortie into France, making a bid for Brittany, Saintonge and the duchy of Gueldres. The careful Scots Parliament refused to vote funds, and ended that venture. He then formed an even more shocking idea, an alliance with England. Naturally this increased his unpopularity still further; Scotland was going through another bout of nostalgia, brought on by circulation of the highly popular verses of Blind Harry about Wallace, who had been hung, drawn and quartered by the English nearly a couple of hundred years before but was not forgotten. The French were affronted too, by the Scots' attempt to gain a foothold in Brittany, and to desert the auld alliance. James's plans broke down and a short brisk campaign between the Scots and English restored the status quo; the English gained Berwick, the disputable fortress, and went home. The king's brother, Earl of Albany, made a bid for the throne, but James III eventually had him exiled to France.

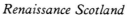

King James IV

'The Thrissle and Rois'

James IV just escaped the customary minority; he was 15 in 1488 at his father's death at Sauchieburn, and he was in the hands of the earls of Angus and Argyll. When he took power he reaffirmed the auld alliance with France, joining with it

King Hans of Denmark, his mother's kinsman. In England power was still uneasy, though the York and Lancaster wars had ended when Henry VII seized the crown of England. James IV promoted the rather ridiculous claims of Perkin Warbeck to the throne of England, a gratuitous piece of aggravation. Eventually, with considerable help from the Pope, the treaty of friendship his father had proposed in 1474 was signed, in 1502, as a Treaty of Perpetual Peace between England and Scotland. The treaty was sealed in the usual way, by a royal wedding. In 1503 James IV married Margaret Tudor, elder sister of the future Henry VIII. The court of Scotland made the best of it, and an elaborate masque was performed with music, song and dance for the occasion, celebrating 'The Thrissle and Rois', at the marriage ceremony in Edinburgh.

> The merle scho sang 'Hail, Rois of most delyt
> Hail of all flouris quene and soverane . . .[1]

[1] The black bird she sang: 'Hail Rose of most delight
Hail, of all flowers queen and sovereign . . .

54

Scotland under James IV and James V reached a high level of internal control, international influence and of placid country life. Poets were given freedom to sing and to criticize, painters made portraits and altarpieces in the manner of the Dutch, Frenchmen rebuilt the palaces in sturdy vernacular versions of Loire chateaux. Dunbar listed the court hangers-on of James IV's day in a wry piece complaining of his own lack of royal patronage:

> Schir ye have mony servitouris
> and officiaris of dyvers curis
> Kirkmen, courtmen and craftismen fyne;
> Doctoris in jure and medicyne;
> Divinouris, rethoris and philosophoris
> Astrologis, artistis and oratoris;
> Men of armes and vailyeand knychtis;
> and mony uther gudlie wichtis;
> Musicians, menstrals and mirrie singaris;
> Chevalouris, carwandaris and carpentaris
> Beildaris of barkis and ballingaris;
> Masounis lyand upon the land,
> and schipwrightis hewand upon the strand
> Glasing wrichtis goldsmythis, and lapidaris
> Pryntouris, payntouris, and potingaris;
> and all of their craft cunning . . .[2]
>
> William Dunbar

[2] Sir, you have many servants, officials of various offices
Churchmen, courtiers and craftsmen fine
Doctors of law and medicine
Seers, speechmakers, philosophers
Astrologers, artists and orators
Men of arms and valiant knights
And many other goodly wights
Musicians, minstrels and merry singers
Chevaliers, cordwainers and carpenters
Builders of two kinds of ship
Masons building on the land
And shipwrights hewing on the beach
Glaziers, goldsmiths and jewellers
Printers, painters and apothecaries
All skilful in their crafts . . .

King James V and an unknown nobleman

Dunbar also compared 'stinking Stirling' to the douce delights of Edinburgh, when James IV was indulging in penances with the Black Friars of Stirling. James was a great man for a pilgrimage, and one of his favourite shrines was that of St Duthac of Tain, which took him journeying to Ross many times. He learned a little Gaelic and understood the proud strong men of the north-west far better than his successors. Mackenzies died with him at Flodden.

Court and country

There were other diversions at court, for example the Abbot of Tongland, a holy conman who claimed to be able to fly. Eventually he protested too much and was forced to the proof; he launched himself from the battlements of Stirling Castle and was retrieved from the deep, soft and humming dung-heap at the foot of the walls. With some presence of mind he claimed that an enemy had substituted hens' feathers for the noble eagles' feathers in his wings, but he was discredited, protesting that of course hens don't fly, by a laughing court. He may have heard of Leonardo da Vinci's theories of flight: Scotland was a fine mix of the sophisticated and the simple. The life of the country folk had altered very little. Agricultural practices were unchanged, and each lord's holding or burgh's lands made up a unit, providing its own policing and law enforcement through hereditary jurisdictions and reluctantly paying such taxes as were demanded by the government. The owner still took his cut in kind: grain and beasts. Over fifty new burghs were established in the second half of the fifteenth century.

Military service was an obligation seldom exacted, though the sheriffs still occasionally drilled the able men in basic military skills; Sheriffmuir near Stirling still marks one such drill ground. The church was made up of extremes, of great wealth in the cathedrals and town centres where corporate piety was expressed in holy guilds, and in oratories for prayers for the dead. At Rosslyn for example, a flamboyant gothic oratory chapel was built which has few equals in fifteenth-century Europe. But at the other end of the spectrum the plain and bare country kirks were served by ill-educated and impoverished clergy, who gained a pittance while the endowed wealth went to monasteries and to city-dwelling clerics, or to laymen who were beginning to help themselves to the rents of richer benefices. The king used church revenues for secular purposes, setting a bad example. Lay abbots scooped most of the income from rich foundations heavily endowed by past piety. At Inchmahome the small Augustinian house of Canons on the beautiful island site in the midst of the Lake of Menteith became 'commended' to the lay hands of the local magnate, Erskine of Cardross. The work of the Canons went on, much hampered by lack of funds. And merchants returning from the Low Countries brought translations of books and scurrilous verses attacking the church and the abuse of her Christian duty by the rich priests and laity. Above all they brought the New Testament, which was eagerly read and circulated. The English translations had been made by Englishmen, and the strong influence of the Bible on national life also strongly influenced the use and development of language; Scots idioms disappeared from print, though not from speech.

The Abbot of Tongland

Flodden Field

James IV's marriage to Margaret Tudor was not particularly happy personally, though dynastically important. Quite soon after her brother Henry became King of England in 1509 the Scots through antipathy to the English were drawn (and not for the only time in Stewart history) into joining a European league against England. James IV proposed a crusade against the Turk. Nothing, in his view, would unite Catholic Europe better, for Islam was on the march, though not quite at the yetts (gates) of Scotland. Unfortunately the rulers of Europe were disinclined to unite, only France and the Holy See urged James forward. France had her standard good reason for the encouragement of Scotland, for in 1513 Henry VIII invaded France, so a diversion on his northern border was valuable for France. It was disastrous for Scotland. James declared war, and the good folk of the realm supported him. Years of peace had if anything made them more bellicose. James sent most of his artillery to France, and took the road south where Surrey was coming up with the second-string English army. They met at Flodden Field in Northumberland. There were killed along with the king eleven earls, three bishops, fifteen lords, hundreds of Scotsmen.

Flodden was a traumatic shock. Nearly three centuries later Jane Elliott vowed she could still bring a tear to the eye over it, and wrote 'The Flowers of the Forest' to prove it.

> The Flowers of the Forest, that fought aye the foremost
> The prime o' our land, are cauld in the clay.

The regents of James V

Flodden was a pointless battle fought for an ungrateful ally. It did not give France any advantage, it did not do much to change the hostility of the English, it was a terrible blow to the realm of Scotland. The subsequent minority and regency during James V's childhood again gave the nobility of Scotland time to regroup, to govern in the name of the infant king by a rough sort of consensus that the strongest nobles would keep the royal child, and power. The life of these infant heirs was always well guarded; it was generally recognized that far worse disorder would arise from a disputed succession in the event of the death of a child king. Certainly, minorities encouraged ruffianly independence amongst the nobles; possibly reliance on the laws of Scotland was also encouraged. In an age where despots on the pattern of the Habsburgs and the French kings were beginning to dominate Europe, a weak king and an independent (if self-seeking) nobility was not a bad thing, and the growth of a competent professional class, using laws and drawn from the small gentry, was even better.

The obvious regent for the king was his mother Queen Margaret Tudor. She resembled her brother Henry VIII in matrimonial adventures, but did not have his eye for political or dynastic justification. She married Archibald Douglas, Earl

The grim harvest of Flodden Field

King James V

of Angus, briefly and tempestuously. The house of Douglas always had plenty of opponents, and Angus's regency did not last long, like his marriage.

Albany, cousin of James IV, was recalled from France and became regent—he could only speak French and was naturally much in favour of renewing the auld alliance, which he did through the Treaty of Rouen. Albany lacked finesse in dealing with the great families, and alienated the Borders by dealing harshly with the leading Homes. In times of hostility with England the Border lords were more independent even than usual: the country had to pay for defence by permitting Border lawlessness. The other leading Border family, the Douglases, naturally were hostile to Albany who had ousted their earl from the regency and stopped up the flow of patronage and easy money which he had directed towards his family. Queen Margaret tried to have her marriage annulled, so she could marry her new love, Henry Stewart.

Under Albany an unsuccessful effort was made to revive hostilities with England on France's behalf; Albany then retired baffled to France, and came back only briefly. The young king grew up, and was taken virtually prisoner by the Douglas faction under his stepfather the Earl of Angus. In 1528 he broke loose and assumed his personal rule, and took stern measures against the Douglases.

James V's rule

Henry VIII did not give up his hostility to the Scots, but mostly was content to huff and puff beyond the border; the few matches played in this league (up to the Battle of Solway Moss) were halfhearted. Henry was in deep trouble of his own with the Pope and the Catholic kings of Europe over the matter of his divorce and the English reformation. The young King of Scotland became a desirable ally once more, in many eyes. The Pope suggested his own niece Catherine de Medici as a possible bride, but that strongminded girl preferred to stay abroad. James had his eye on Madeleine, daughter of the King of France, Francis I. After a few more turns of the political merry-go-round he did marry Madeleine, but seven months later she was dead, and James was grief-stricken. He had begun to rebuild Falkland Palace, the most intimate and elegant Stewart palace, for her. It was completed for her successor Marie of Guise, perhaps the most influential Queen of Scotland since Margaret the wife of Ceanmhor. Uncle Henry VIII was not amused, he had been considering marrying Marie of Guise himself.

James V was strongly acquisitive, and enforced all the old feudal dues on his mightier subjects, raising large sums from them on a number of legal or semi-legal pretexts. He did not call his Parliaments so often either, preferring to govern through a convocation, a less formal gathering of notables, and through his Privy Council. Those whom he ceased to trust soon lost more than the royal favour, their lands were often forfeited too. James V looked first to the church to supply him with funds. In 1532 he founded the College of Justice, a fine-sounding rationalization of existing arrangements with the Court of Session. He raised £10,000 Scots from a personal tax on the bishops of Scotland to fund it. To live magnificently, as a Renaissance ruler was expected to do, cost money. James hoarded gold in odd corners, for emergencies, or for visits abroad, and Albany received a stream of instructions about the expected dowries of James's two

French brides. The lands of troublesome nobles were forfeited to the crown, and the crown feued out the lands of its own on high terms. Henry VIII constantly pointed out to his nephew that his own solution of dissolving the monasteries had proved extremely profitable: James, however, preferred to maintain the church as a convenient milch-cow, by writing sycophantic letters to the Pope saying he was doing his best to keep heresy out of Scotland, and at the same time putting in outrageous demands for his nine illegitimate children. 'The royal dignity of the boy will put a restraint upon the impious,' he remarked with—apparently—a straight face when seeking the Pope's permission to make a six-year-old child prior of St Andrew's Abbey.

Church and folk

Sir David Lindsay, licensed court poet and old friend of the king since the royal childhood, wrote a splendid satire for Twelfth Night at Linlithgow Palace in 1540, *Ane Satire of the Thrie Estaitis*, in which his hero, John the Commonweal, complains about many things: the problems of gaining common justice, the burden of taxation, the corruption of the church.

> 'This poor commons daily as ye may see
> Declinis down to extreme poverty . . .'

Oppression, he said, weakens the realm

> 'I pray you sir,
> Begin first at the Border
> For how can we feud us agains England
> When we can not within our native land
> Destroy our own Scots Common traitor theives,
> Wha to leil labourere daily does mischieves?'

The worst traitors were the

> 'Great fat freirs
> Augustines Carmelites and Cordeleins
> And all others that in Cowls been clead
> Whilk laboures not, and been weill fed.'

Lindsay lays about him, criticizing parish priests who took the widow's last cow for funeral dues, and bishops who 'flew in riches royally', and one of his characters, 'Flattery', is shocked to be handed a book by 'Verity': 'This is the New Testament. In Inglis tongue and prentit in England! Heresy, Heresy! Fire, Fire incontinuent!'

A generation before the formal break with Rome the signs of the new Protestant movement were plain to behold. The Scots in the burghs were more inclined towards Protestant beliefs than were the countrymen at this point. Burgesses were in a position to read the heretical literature that was smuggled in from England and the Low Countries. They also could observe the excesses of the great prelates and the elaboration of services in the great churches and

monasteries. In the country the simple folk had no great grip of theology, and their kirks were apt to be bare, and clergy penurious. Though they had a grasp of the essentials of Christianity it was apt to be mixed up with residual cults of holy wells, singing heads and the recited charms for sickness which were characteristic of a pre-literate society. Most of the people of Scotland were strongly based in oral traditions, mistrustful of the few men who were literate, the great, the merchants and clerics. The 'little culture' of the Scottish folk was powerful and tenacious, existing below the literate level. This oral culture fitted in well with the Roman church which operated through ritual and repetition, and which was soon to be opposed by the plain services and the emphasis on reading the Bible and on literacy which characterized the Protestant Reformation. It was a deep clash, one of the causes of the witchcraft obsession which later disfigured the seventeenth century in Scotland. Witches were equated with the half-forgotten half-pagan world existing before the establishment of the Reformed Church. The genuine piety of the Middle Ages however should not be questioned: without some grasp of the basic tenets of the Christian faith it is doubtful if the demands of the Renaissance Papacy would have been rejected so briskly for the ornate sham that they had become. The songs collected in the *Carmina Gadelica* show the simplicity of oral Christianity in Scotland.

Ballads, also products of an oral tradition, had an even longer survival than shadowy Celtic beliefs. Ballads are tightly structured and repetitive in standard patterns which, though complicated, carry the memory of the singer through and provide a framework for the making of new songs. This the Scots did with zest and a wide choice of subjects, from ones with roots in legends from old Denmark, Ireland or even classical Greece, to celebrations of local love affairs, battles and murders. Few exactly supply historical evidence, most are difficult to date, most carry the authentic flavour of the Scots peoples. It has been argued that balladmaking is stimulated by racial clashes; certainly in Scotland the two main homes of balladry have been the Borders and, even more, the north-east, where Highlander and Lowlander met often in bloody conflict:

> As I cam in by Dunidier
> An down by Netherha'
> There were fifty thousand Hielanmen
> A-marching to Harlaw . . .

and to the battle which became a byword for Lowland fears of incursions of wild 'Hielanmen'.

Mary and Marie of Guise

The battle of Solway Moss, one of those routine engagements between the Scots and the English, was fought in 1542. James V had left his Queen Marie of Guise to bear a child at Linlithgow Palace; in four years of marriage two sons had died in infancy. The heavy Scots defeat at Solway Moss threw James into a mysterious but fatal decline; he turned his face to the wall in his little painted chamber at Falkland and died soon after he heard his wife had been delivered of a bonny girl.

Mary was Queen of Scots at the end of her first week of age, and power was never far from the control of her patient clever mother Marie of Guise during her minority. Marie of Guise had to allow the indignity of having her child stripped naked under the hard probing hands of the English ambassador, who had heard the child was sickly. Still worse, she had to endure the regency of James Hamilton, Earl of Arran and Duc de Châtelhérault in France. Hamilton had noble birth and every attribute for a successful regency except one; like his forebears he could seldom make up his mind. Marie of Guise, holding Scotland for her absent daughter whom she sent to her family in France, led an upright lonely life, unlike the last widowed queen Margaret Tudor, whose conduct was fairly scandalous. But Marie was vainly swimming against the tide, which was setting fair for the Protestants of the realm. Politics and religion could never be disentangled, in the sixteenth century least of all. Marie wanted to keep the auld alliance between her own country, France, and Scotland, but while Mary Tudor was on the throne of England it was necessary for Marie of Guise to encourage the Protestants, to avoid Scotland ending up in the militantly Catholic arms of the Queen of England.

The years 1558-60 were ones of fast-moving events. In the spring of 1558 Mary Queen of Scots' marriage with the Dauphin of France was celebrated. Mary Tudor

died and the English acknowledged her half-sister, Elizabeth, queen. In Catholic eyes Mary Queen of Scots was the legitimate heir, not Henry VIII's bastard daughter of an illegal marriage, Elizabeth. Marie of Guise persuaded the Parliament of Scotland to give her daughter's husband Francis the Crown Matrimonial; the accidental death of his father then made him King of France as well as King of Scotland. Elizabeth, whose Protestant leanings were reinforced by Catholics questioning her legitimacy and by the open claim of the King and Queen of Scotland and France to the throne of England, encouraged the Scottish Protestants. Never as bellicose as her father, she preferred devious diplomacy, which matched the rather hesitant moves of the Scots nobility. Some of these Elizabeth bought, though the 'English Party' did not always keep her bargain. They were by no means ardent for reformation; however the suggestion, made in the Scots Council of 1559, that the Catholic Church of Scotland should be reformed, and that church property in lay hands should be recovered and the rents devoted to the poor, made most of them Protestants. For at least a couple of generations many great families had enjoyed both the feus and teinds (rents and tithes) of much church land and had no intention of losing such lucrative revenues.

In this year, too, John Knox became minister of the High Kirk of St Giles in Edinburgh, and with his great gift of eloquence swayed city opinion. He neither feared nor flattered princes, and his Calvinism had been learned in Geneva and tempered with a spell as a prisoner pulling an oar in a royal galley of France. He combined a fascination with women 'in their place' with a hatred and fear of their power; queens on the thrones of England and Scotland gave his tongue and pen great scope. Pushed to the extreme, Knox in his *First and Second Blasts of the Trumpet against the Monstrous Regiment of Women* claimed his own right, and that of the reformed leaders of the kirk, to dictate to the monarch. This led to 100 years of strife, with Scotland several times on the brink of theocracy, the temporal rule of the ministers of the kirk (backed by town crowds). Fortunately, though, the innate common sense of the country prevailed against the rule of those would-be ayatollahs of Presbyterianism. By 1560 Queen Elizabeth's English armies had marched about, the Scots had avoided direct engagements and the few French troops of the Queen Regent had done well. Public opinion in Scotland, forced to choose between a French Catholic alliance or an English Protestant one, veered decisively towards the English. The 'semi-legal baronial pressure-group, the self-chosen Lords of the Congregation', as the alliance of nobles has been well described, acted with the divines to establish the Protestant Church. Already Knox and a crowd had destroyed the churches and friaries of Perth in a night of riot and fire, and

the Lords of Congregation were tacitly with them. The Reformed Church began, though, peacefully and by popular agreement; nearly all the priests stayed on as ministers, so there was little blood shed, and hardly any martyrs. More 'Romish' buildings were later destroyed by Cromwell's army than by Knox's reformers.

Elizabeth's captain-general negotiated the Treaty of Berwick with the Lords of Congregation; this safeguarded the English queen's claim to her own throne, rejected the French alliance and the Catholic Church, and opened the gates to a Protestant Church of Scotland. Marie of Guise died of a heart ailment, knowing her policy was totally ruined, through lack of enough French support as much as for Scottish hostility. In August 1560 Parliament met, with a Protestant majority, accepted the Protestant Confession of Faith, and commissioned *The Book of Discipline* whose provisions, amongst much else, repeated the suggestion that the laity should return the church lands, to provide for the education of the poor and the new clergy. This again was highly unpopular, but a working bargain was eventually struck.

Mary in Scotland

In the autumn of 1561 Mary returned to Scotland. She was a widow of 18, a tall, impetuous girl, with none of her cousin Elizabeth's political subtlety, and with the fatal Stewart facility for choosing the wrong men as her intimates. Fortunately at the start of her reign she had her half-brother Lord James Stewart and Maitland of Lethington at her side. With them, she wanted to preserve the liberty of worship for both Catholic and Protestant in her kingdom, and this then appeared feasible. She remained personally Catholic. Her remarriage became politically important. There was a handy candidate, the brainless handsome Henry Lord Darnley, cousin of both queens, Protestant and not involved with any foreign power. Mary fell for his looks, and only later discovered his obstinate stupidity. The marriage quickly ran into dificulties, and Darnley and some ruffianly nobles killed the queen's secretary Rizzio almost at her feet, out of jealousy. In spite of such shocks Mary gave birth to her only living child, James, three months later, and her marriage was saved, on the surface. But Henry Darnley sulked, he wanted 'the Crown Matrimonial', he was impossible. The queen found him impossible. The house in which he was staying at Kirk o' Fields was blown up by gunpowder in a murky plot which benefited Mary, though she was probably not the instigator. She was at the time wildly in love with the most ruffianly of her court, James Hepburn, Earl of Bothwell, a man even less acceptable to the Scots people than Darnley had been. It was seen all at once that Mary herself was not necessary. The infant James was safely in the hands of the Earl and Countess of Mar, and if Mary were eliminated the great game of a royal minority could be played again, with a Protestant princeling assured at the end.

IV
James VI and I

The king's minority

MARY WAS imprisoned on an island in Loch Leven in 1567, where she was put under such pressure by the nobility that she abdicated in favour of her infant son James. So, in 1568, Mary's star set. The young king was to be raised a Protestant in accordance with the general wish of the kingdom. Regent Moray, bastard of James V and so half-brother to Queen Mary, ruled with one eye peeled for the conspiracies of Hamilton, who was legitimate and had a good claim to the throne. Mary escaped from Leven, but the Hamilton family as usual vacillated, and eventually gave her no support. From a hostile Scotland she fled over the border as a refugee to England. This posed a severe strain on her cousin Elizabeth, who did not want to encourage any ideas of displacing queens regnant, nor did she want the diplomatic problem which Mary represented. Mary was still only in her twenties, a tall hard-riding impulsive girl, lacking judgement. Elizabeth kept her under house arrest. Regent Moray was shot dead in 1570 by one of the Hamilton party, and Scottish politics polarized into king's men and queen's men, though as one nominal leader was a child and the other an absent prisoner the division was theoretical only.

Elizabeth as usual hated to disclose her interest but she supported the new regent Morton, who had an eight-year rule. He was tough, with past direct involvement in the death of Rizzio and possibly that of Darnley, the king's father. He was strong on law and order, he refortified Edinburgh Castle, made unpopular attempts to control the Border barons, and ineffectual ones to control price rises and inflation. As one of his ideas was to mint more money the Scots pound slipped from being worth about a quarter of the pound sterling to only one-twelfth by 1600, a position it held for the next 107 years until the Union of Parliaments extinguished the Scots pound for ever.

Nor had the religious settlement been made with any permanency. Bishops, nominated by the crown and confirmed by the Assembly, continued to officiate, rather on the English pattern. The finances of the kirk were inadequate and insecure; the wealth of the Catholic Church had gone into lay pockets for some time past. Organization within the kirk was still fluid. Meantime James VI grew up mainly in Stirling, of which Mar was custodian. Lady Mar gave him a good start in life but the schoolmasters soon took him over. He often stayed for quite long periods in the Stewart castle of Doune, where the air was thought better. He had long and stiff lessons, and became a good Latinist by his eighth year. His tutor was the formidable scholar George Buchanan, and he had a few schoolboys in class with him, including a whipping boy, a medieval survival which probably met with the young king's approval. Not that James was a naughty child, he seems to have been eager to learn and informal with his subjects, and he developed the love of language which had characterized his ancestors. He too was a poet, but unfortunately he was raised in a pedantic school and his poetry is indifferent. However, few kings of Britain have expressed themselves in verse or published books since. James VI cannot have had a happy childhood, so perhaps it was fortunate that he had a taste for books. His mother was in the custody of Elizabeth of England until he was 20 years old; Elizabeth then reluctantly beheaded her. James had never known her, and had been taught to despise her and fear her Catholic adherents. James was said to be physically unattractive, a hard worker and full of enthusiasms, and (perhaps like James III) frightened of armed men and drawn swords. There had been plenty of those in his childhood. Soon after his majority he fell in love with a useless young kinsman whom he made Duke of Lennox; then he was betrothed to Anne, the King of Denmark's daughter, and nearly bankrupted the treasury with the fine showing he and his court made at the royal wedding in Copenhagen. He feared witches, and believed a coven had conspired to raise a storm on his return to Leith with his bride.

James VI and I

The prospect of England

James VI lived all his reign under the increasing expectation of being acknowledged heir to the throne of England. However, Queen Elizabeth was secretive, and reluctant to discuss death and heirs; there was only a presumption, although his claim to the throne of England was good. It was derived from his great-grandmother Margaret Tudor's marriage to James IV, from whom his descent was direct, and the claim was reinforced by his father Henry Lord Darnley, also a grandson of Margaret Tudor (his parents were first cousins). The Tudors had left few descendants. But an impeccable claim was all that it was.

All his adult life James had the glittering prospect of England before him, with its great riches and prestige, but no certainty of inheriting. Prudent Elizabethan statesmen such as Cecil had corresponded with him, and he tried to prepare himself and his eldest son for possible new responsibilities. His book *Basilikon Doron* was a kind of handbook for princes, written for the guidance of Henry his son, and became eagerly read by English and foreign ambassadors, in the hope of assessing the mind of the possible new King of England.

James VI in Scotland

James VI was an able king and made strenuous efforts to improve the justice and administration of Scotland, and to increase overseas trade. Unfortunately his efforts for the latter merely increased inflation, through depreciation of the currency. Coal mining increased, commercial fishing expanded a little. The salt pans were extended as demand for salt to preserve the fish of the sea was great. Trade across the North Sea slowly expanded, and round the Baltic shores every small trader or pedlar was called 'Scottis' as a generic description. Although efforts were made to improve Scottish standards of manufacture, much was still imported. Swedish pig iron came to the smiddies (smithies) of Scotland whose main products were household goods and the great iron yetts, the gates and window-bars with which prudent men still secured their entrances. Little iron was demanded for agricultural tools, which were mostly of wood tipped with iron. Munitions of war still had to be purchased abroad. James's rule of Scotland was shrewd, personal and efficient, and made use of the emerging class of lay professional servants of the crown.

Elizabeth of England died in 1603, and James was summonsed to her vacant place. He, followed by Queen Anne and their servants, bundled together their best clothes and hurried down the Great North Road as fast as the lumbering coaches of the day would go. The palaces of Holyrood House, Stirling, Linlithgow and Falkland all stood empty, and all the minor officials of the court—the falconers, the mistresses of the robes and lords of the tapestry, the cooks and grooms and embroiderers went onto board wages. The king's limner had no portraits to paint, the historiographer royal had a pension, but little to record. The royal focus of the country had shifted 400 miles to the south. James took only a few of his staff, including his Scots physician.

King James VI

The lack of a court did not have an immediate effect on the country which continued to prosper in an undramatic way. The towns grew, benefiting also from the new habit of nobles and gentry to come into the towns for the winter, to little 'town houses', and for the sessions of the Court of Session in Edinburgh or the sheriff courts of the countryside. Their younger sons became lawyers, their dependants became ministers of the kirk, and everyone with any money bought a little land, and had a few trading ventures. The landowners of the north-east, for example, sold bere barley to the brewers of Edinburgh, or encouraged flax-growing and weaving. The royal children, Henry Prince of Wales, his stuttering shy brother Charles, Elizabeth their sister, the 'Dochter of Scotland', occasionally were sent for holidays to the half-empty palaces.

The royal Scots in England

The English made some effort to adapt to the royal Scots, and they in turn found the rich Tudor pastures very much to their liking. Buildings, dress and all the luxuries of life were far more lavish than anything found north of the border, and the Scots nobles who came to court found it hard to keep up appearances. The expenditure needed for attendance on the king, in London and on royal progress round the country, was a drain on private Scottish purses and a drawback to political ambition, affecting the functioning of Scottish politics. Queen Anne turned to masques and theatricals, King James fell in love with a pretty page boy whom he eventually made Duke of Buckingham, and one of the court actors wrote a play which he hoped would please the new king. He scoured old chronicles for a suitable Scottish setting, and brought in a strong flavour of witchcraft which was known to fascinate King James. *Macbeth* is perhaps the ultimate study in English language of ambition, guilt and power lust.

Shakespeare made, however, a travesty of Scottish history which has distorted the record in that respect ever since.

James's efforts to unite his two kingdoms failed; he had the old Scots concept of the marriage of king with realm, not a part of English tradition which was more pragmatic and legalistic. The Scots, familiar with France and northern Europe, found England very foreign; the English found the Scots uncouth and their language harsh and outlandish. James's efforts to persuade the two nobilities to intermarry were not successful, English heiresses were reluctant to venture north; neither Scots peers nor their impoverished daughters were matrimonial 'catches'. In trade the English feared to be undercut by the Scots with their more thrifty ideas of expenditure. James's schemes for unions, of customs, Parliament and of church, all failed, and each country remained independent and aloof.

The General Assemblies of the kirk were a possible threat to the crown of Scotland, but James acted with firmness, even imprisoning or banishing ministers who showed too much independence. Most independent was Andrew Melville, Principal of Glasgow University, who advocated the supremacy of the kirk, coupled with a strong antipathy towards bishops. He incurred the king's displeasure. James began by controlling the extremes of presbyterian opinion, and restoring the eroded status of bishops in the kirk, without much opposition. But after some years in England his opinions leaned more to English ways. He began to formulate the doctrine of the divine right of kings.

He returned only once to Scotland, in 1617, and then pushed through a set of new regulations for the kirk, reintroducing the main festivals of the Christian year and other Anglican notions. James's popularity waned a little, though his control was still strong. The Scots Parliament dutifully endorsed the legalisation

the king sent up, and the Privy Council, enlarged to a Convention, with the royal office bearers, chancellor, secretary and treasurer, ran the country according to the king's behests.

Lowlands and Highlands

The crown did not entirely control the people in one important area, that of blood feuds. The Lowland Scots were beginning to turn to law to settle claims. Though men of the same name still tended to act in unison they seldom sallied out armed to attack their neighbours. The properly conducted blood feud, or the bond to end one, was still acknowledged as a means of settling disputes. The personal authority of the lord as head of the family was invoked, and relied on by the king. 'Benorth the Forth', where at least half the total population of Scotland lived, disputes were more often settled with the sword. It was at this period that the clan MacGregor's violations of law and order were so notable and bloody that James proscribed the clan altogether. Their territory was on the edge of the Lowlands, good grazing for which they forcibly recruited their neighbours' cattle. Further north and west the royal strategy was to put policing into the

hands of the most powerful of the clans, to act in the king's name. But the islands still were intractable to royal rule based on Central Scotland. The decline of the MacDonald lords of the Isles had left an imbalance in north-west Scotland.

James VI made the first of many subsequent attempts to impose a colonial solution to the problem posed by the inhabitants of the Islands, who were poor, proud quarrelsome Gaels, still with a Celtic culture and society which did not accord with the rest of Scotland, and still with an inclination to the old Catholic faith. Like many colonialists James VI was convinced that he acted in the best interest of the whole country, and his solution took the two classic forms of drastic educational and economic reform. Under royal orders Bishop Knox of the Isles took ship to western waters, and after nearly a year of negotiating with the leaders (whom he had secured on board his ship) the Statutes of Iona were signed on the holy island of Iona. The provisions were a direct attempt to subordinate Gaelic culture and to substitute a bland pan-Scottish uniformity. The leaders were asked to keep the king's law, to support the Reformed Church in worship and by the payment of ministers' stipends, to send their eldest sons to school in the Lowlands, to abstain from feuding and to disarm, and to dismiss their bards, pipers and sennachies. (Gaelic was no longer to be considered the language of gentlemen.)

These provisions did improve the keeping of law and order in the lawless west, but struck a severe blow at Gaelic culture and learning. Along with the blood feuds went music and song, good metal work, Latin learning, and medical knowledge as good as anywhere in Scotland. The physicians of the MacBeath clan, the Beatons (or the 'Sons of Life') of Mull, for example, owned Gaelic manuscripts and herbals so precious and so up-to-date by sixteenth-century standards that the doctor's ghillie had to run round the head of the loch with the books while the doctor took the more dangerous ferry.

76

The second measure taken by James VI to bring the Islands into the kingdom was even more overtly colonial. Taking advantage of the longstanding feuding between MacLeod of Lewis and Mackenzie of Kintail, in 1600 he authorized the forfeit of the Island of Lewis and formation of a Royal Company of Merchant Adventurers of Fife, who were to take it over, develop its fisheries and turn it into a granary. Although the Fife Adventurers succeeded in founding the town of Stornoway their venture totally failed, leaving the Mackenzies in control of Lewis, from which island their leader took title as Earl of Seaforth when King James advanced him. Seaforth made quite a sensation at court in England with his tall Mackenzie good looks, his Highland dress and courtly manners. He was a good example of the risks of court life—he was perpetually hard up. Lewis was left no better off. The house of Argyll was in some disarray in James VI's time, but still received royal favour and commissions of the peace which enabled Campbells to absorb their neighbours' lands under legal pretexts. In the east and in Sutherland the Gordons kept state, the Cocks of the North.

James also had to reimpose central control over the Orkneys, where his mother had allowed her kinsman Patrick Earl of Orkney to rule and plunder unchecked. The recruiting of Scotsmen for the army of England had begun. Scotland had no standing army of her own, nor had the English, except in times of danger. This was to change.

James should be remembered for many things, but on one count alone he did well for the unity of his two kingdoms. The Authorized Version of the Bible completed by scholars working at the king's command, went into every English and Scottish home, and gave unity and a common ground not only to religious thought but to language and expression, for generations to come.

God and the state

From the time of James V up to quite recent times the strongest strand in Scottish life was a twin preoccupation with religion and politics. The relationship between the Reformed kirk, and the king and civil government, was first debated during Mary's reign, and formed an undercurrent throughout the reign of James VI and his son Charles I. The Civil Wars brought the debate to warfare, and we shall see a period when the Covenanting kirk was in the ascendant and ruled the country. Concern over the relationship of kirk and state continued through the Commonwealth period, and became acute again during the Restoration of Charles II when the pendulum swung back to episcopacy. William of Orange's Protestant settlement established the Presbyterian Church of Scotland, but this was by no means acceptable to all Scots; dissatisfaction with it contributed to subsequent Jacobite risings, up to 1746. Philosophers of the Scottish Enlightenment of the later years of the eighteenth century gave a humanist and rationalist turn to the debate, but the strictly domestic and theological question still existed and gave rise to the secession churches that broke away from the

Established church, culminating in the great Disruption of 1843, a last flicker of the old fiery dilemma between man's duty to God and his duty to the state.

This was always the underlying preoccupation, the great question posed all over Europe and answered in varying ways by the Reformation. The question concerned the nature of government and its legal authority, and the relationship of the individual to his environment: man as a single unit living within the state. This is the political side of the coin, the reverse of the theological side, man's relationship to God. The Protestant Reformation, stemming from Luther, Calvin and the Geneva divines, enunciated two great principles of political thought: firstly the duty of free inquiry, including access to the Scriptures, secondly the priesthood of all believers. The first led to liberty in a political as well as a religious sense through the need to form independent judgements; the second to the equality of all men in a political sense, as well as postulating that man needs no intermediary (or priest) to approach God.

In Scotland, hitherto so dependent on the oral tradition, the opening of Scripture was enormously important and formative. The duty and the pleasure of reading the Bible in every home enjoined by Knox's *Book of Discipline*, and gradually but widely achieved, not only coloured all religious thinking but caused a great upsurge in general literacy. The doors were open to religious, political and moral speculation.

With liberty of conscience in the Reformed church came the thorny question of the legality of government. Calvin, whose influence on Wishaw and Knox, the architects of the Scottish Reformation, was initially great, was firm—but essentially contradictory—on this point. In his *Institutes*, in an important chapter

'On Civil Government', he wrote about the dual obedience to the spiritual kingdom of Christ and to civil government which man must offer. Because civil government and laws of the land are necessary, obedience is necessary but—and it is a big but—there is a right of resistance if obedience to the state is incompatible with God's laws. And every man in the Reformed church was the keeper of his own conscience. Calvin left the question open. Knox had to face it in a more practical form: was obedience to a Catholic ruler, as Mary Queen of Scots was, a duty to the Protestant subject, or not? Knox took the hard line and in his *Second Blast* declared that 'No oath can bind the people to obey and maintain tyrants against God.' For over a generation the Scots people had hated the corrupt Renaissance Papacy, and had seen the Pope of Rome as their worst enemy, as Antichrist or Lucifer. The popular songs of the day demonstrate this. A collection of *Gude and Godlie Ballatis* first circulated about 1540 and for long after. Among demotic versions of psalms and other devotional verses are a few more racy ones which fitted jolly popular tunes, such as:

> The hunter is Christ, that huntis in haist
> The hundis ar Peter and Paull,
> The Paip is the fox, Rome is the rox
> That rubbis us on the gall . . .

Scotland was not alone in the dilemma of a ruler with a different faith to the people. In the Spanish Netherlands long bloody wars eventually led to the founding of the United Provinces, free of Spain. Huguenots in France eventually failed to obtain toleration. In 1620 the example of the English Pilgrim Fathers who sought to found a state in America based on religious contract was noted. Soon after Mary's exile in England the scholar-tutor to the young king, George Buchanan, wrote *De Jure Regni* in impeccable Latin, to justify her deposition. His sentiments were so strongly in favour of the people's right to withdraw obedience from any civil ruler whom they cannot in conscience respect that his book was actually burnt in Oxford over a hundred years later, when James VII and II had come full circle and was once again providing the problem of a Catholic prince to the Protestant peoples of two kingdoms. But much had happened in that century.

Charles I, though born in Scotland, was brought up in England, and never felt at home with Scots. He inherited Scotland in quite a peaceful though not a very prosperous state. Famines still hit different areas, and affected the poor worst of all, but there was also some slow economic advance. This was naturally especially noticeable in the merchant class in the burghs: these began to improve their comforts and to acquire better household graith—or goods. It was these men who strongly supported the presbyterian order. The keeping of the Sabbath began to become one of the most important distinguishing marks of the good Presbyterian, though the old cheerful celebrations of the great feasts of the church took a long time to disappear.

King Charles II after his Restoration

V

Religion and War

CHARLES I came to grief in the debate between the divine right of an absolute monarch and the free consciences of his Puritan and presbyterian subjects in both kingdoms. It was a long, complex and agonizing debate. Charles became increasingly autocratic, and increased taxation in both kingdoms. He attempted once more to give the Church of Scotland an adequate financial base by a fairer share of the old lands formerly belonging to the Catholic Church. After some years of acrimonious negotiation a reasonable settlement was worked out: nobles in possession kept the lands, paid crown rents and gave over the teinds (tithes) for the support of the church. Those holding former church lands had also to give up various protected privileges. Naturally there was dissatisfaction, which contributed to the Great Rebellion of the three kingdoms, touched off in Scotland.

It was more of a crisis of confidence and of conscience than anything else. Charles came belatedly, in 1633, to be crowned in Scotland, supported by a full retinue of English bishops to stiffen the ill-regulated Scots bishops who were little more than superintendents of presbyteries, neither much resented nor much heeded up to this point. Archbishop Laud even instructed them in how to dress. Charles was a tidy, orderly man and thought English church ordinances were quite simply the best and most suitable for both his realms. He caused the Scottish bishops to produce a new Prayer Book, a Liturgy. He had already alienated the Scots Parliament, and the Liturgy was considered the last straw.

Charles, back in London, seriously underestimated the strength of opposition in Scotland. In February 1638 the leaders of the opposition in Scotland drew up the National Covenant, an immensely long legalistic document which rehearsed all the old arguments and rejected all innovations, such as the new Prayer Book. It ended by demanding a free Parliament and General Assembly of the kirk, in language dominated by Old Testament accounts of Jehovah's pact with Israel, the Chosen People. Public subscription to the Covenant was widespread, difficult indeed to escape as signature was public. Possibly with some misgivings, the greater part of the gentry and citizenry of Scotland signed the Covenanting Band. Though not unlike the bands often entered into by rebellious nobles against the king in the past, this band had a new feature, taking the name of God into the compact itself. The Covenant thus meant that the Scots went to war against the king ('the Malignant'), convinced that the Lord was with them, and therefore their lack of munitions or of battle plans was not important. The Lord would provide.

General Leslie came back from long service in the Protestant armies of Europe, and Montrose and other nobles, including the young Earl of Argyll, declared for the Covenant. An Assembly was held in Glasgow in open defiance of the king and bishops. Soon a Scottish Covenanting army was chasing the king's men out of the royal strongholds of Edinburgh, Dumbarton and Dalkeith. By the time they reached Berwick Charles was ready to negotiate a settlement agreeing to call a Scots Parliament and an Assembly. The Scots were confirmed in their belief that God was on their side. By 1640 they were sure of it, and went to war again, claiming that bishops were obnoxious and should be rooted out of both England and Scotland—thus directly challenging royal authority in the righteous spirit that an unjust ruler should be resisted. Montrose brilliantly led the Covenanting forces to victory across the Tweed, and Charles was forced to recall the English Parliament and to agree to pay the Scots army.

Charles, the Cavaliers and Covenanters

Back in Scotland a fevered enthusiasm for the righteous cause grew, but the leaders of the army fell out. Montrose struggled with his conscience, and turned against Argyll because of his attack on the castle of Airlie, belonging to Montrose's kin, in the course of a policing commission in the east:

> Lady Margaret looks o'er her bower window
> And O but she looks weary.
> And there she spied the great Argyll
> Coming to plunder the bonny house of Airly . . .

It was a great age for balladmaking. For all this disagreement (which had later serious results) a commission was sent from the victorious Covenanters to London to treat with the king, and visions of reforming the English and imposing pure presbyterian practices on the 'corrupt' English church floated before Scots' eyes. The English however persisted in considering the matter in a light more political than theological. They debated the king's unjust taxation with more heat. Eventually the English Parliament went far further in its claims of independence and supremacy than the Scots had done. Charles came north to Edinburgh, driven to seek Scottish support, though his manner antagonized many of his Scots friends in the process. He left Scotland neutral, on the sidelines of the Civil War which then broke out between king and English Parliament.

The king's forces, after a year of fighting, looked like winning so the English commissioners went to Scotland for help for the parliamentary side. Late in 1643 the Solemn League and Covenant was drawn up on Scottish terms. The Scots insisted that the agreement between them and the English and Irish should impose a general Presbyterian Church organization. The English Puritans wanted liberty and in religion 'independency' was their watchword. Toleration was not a word favoured in the kirk, and only the strongest draughts of the intoxicating Old Testament could have made the Scots' leaders believe that a presbyterian solution *could* be imposed on England or Ireland. Most of the Irish were royalist as well as Papist and an Irish invasion was a real threat. A large Scots army, well equipped, went south to support English parliamentarians, but played a rather minor and inglorious part in the battle of Marston Moor, a parliamentary victory in which General Cromwell came into prominence. Cromwell was a member of Parliament, and an Independent in religion.

Great Montrose

Meantime some royalist Irish had landed in the west of Scotland, a thousand MacDonald warriors of an old Celtic style, bringing women and cattle in their tail. And, as a worse shock, Montrose had gone out with them, in the king's name. In the autumn and winter of 1644 Montrose led them in a flying column through the Highlands, attacking Argyll's strongpoints and taking the king's colours through the north in a series of brilliant guerilla forays. It was, however, too late; Marston Moor had destroyed the king's chances. Bitter feelings were engendered in Scotland; by opposing the Covenanters Montrose was attacking God, by beating them he caused them to search their souls; how had they failed their Ally—or He them? Montrose was a monarchist of an old-fashioned sort, and his support came mainly from those in the north who mistrusted the extremes of theocratic government and the ascendancy of Argyll. The king's army was then decisively defeated at Naseby; Cromwell and the New Model Army controlled England, and Cromwell favoured neither the Scots nor presbytery. Montrose's successes in the north were still great enough for him to call a Parliament in Scotland in the king's name, and he planned to march on England. His Irish and Highland supporters did not however care to campaign south of the Forth, and melted off to the west, driving cattle. He was defeated in the Borders at Philiphaugh by General Leslie:

> Now let us a' for Lesly pray
> And his brave company,
> For they have vanquished Great Montrose
> Our cruel enemy . . .

Both sides made ballads. Montrose escaped to hide in the Highlands, and the Covenanters took savage reprisals on captured soldiers and supporters.

The English armies purged Scots cathedrals

Charles a prisoner

Charles I suddenly appeared at the camp of the Covenanting Scots' army at Newark, and surrendered to them. For some months after, the ablest Covenanters tried to persuade Charles, under house arrest in Newcastle, to become a Covenanted Presbyterian. Charles listened politely and remained unconvinced. Montrose was still at large in the north, and Huntly had a force in the field for the king, but they were far away. The Scots sold King Charles for the price of half their army's back pay, £200,000, to the English Parliament, and went home. The English army took charge of the king's person, but he sent messages to the Covenanting chiefs 'engaging' to support a presbyterian settlement of England in return for a Scots attack on the Army. Those who rallied were called Engagers. The resulting 'second civil war' did not last long, the Parliamentary Army easily beat the Scots, led ineffectually by Hamilton and Middleton. The more extreme Covenanters then rose up and threw out the Engagers, so that when Cromwell came north he was faced by a minority government of fanatical Presbyterians, who governed by executing or imprisoning any who questioned their authority, that of a theocratic police state. Cromwell shrewdly saw the dangerously strong undercurrent of royalist support in Scotland, and the execution of the king was carried out in January 1649. The English Parliament, just before the execution, formulated the ultimate Protestant position: 'The people are, under God, the origin of all just power . . . The Commons of England in Parliament assembled have supreme power in this nation.'

Scottish opposition to Parliament

Far from this ending the business, the English were astonished to find that the execution of the king had united the Scots in opposition to England. Though for centuries the Scots had tried to browbeat or outwit their monarch, they did not hold with the English executing a king of Scotland. His son was immediately proclaimed king Charles II in Edinburgh, but with the proviso that he must first swear to the Solemn League before being invested. In this confused period Montrose was captured and brought to Edinburgh, with his feet humiliatingly tied together under a pony's belly. He expected no more mercy than the ruling Covenanters had ever shown, and was executed and quartered, along with some of his officers. He wrote, on the eve of execution:

> Let them bestow on ev'ry Airth a Limb . . .
> Lord, since Thou knowest where all these Atoms are
> I'm hopeful, once Thou'lt recollect my Dust
> And confident Thou'lt raise me with the Just.

Charles II reluctantly arrived in Scotland to embrace the Covenant—for wholly political ends—and was preached at by the hour. Cromwell led an army into Scotland. There was much debate before the fight, and Cromwell's words might be taken as a text by all arbitrators in difficult debates: 'I beseech you in the bowels of Christ think it possible that you may be mistaken.' The Covenanters did not think it possible, and outside Dunbar the Scots army was heavily defeated, partly because ministers had rejected many ungodly but experienced old soldiers, and had persisted in giving General Leslie military advice. Cromwell sent many of the prisoners after Dunbar to the West Indies as indentured labour, white slaves. After the defeat of Dunbar the remaining Covenanters were seen to be a political party, occasionally with the new nickname 'Whig' attached, not men who were divine intermediaries. Argyll remained out of sight in the west; a small Whig rising in Ayrshire was put down. Moderate and royalist opinion strengthened, and the Scots still had the person of the king.

Charles II and the battle of Worcester

Charles II was crowned King of Scots at Scone, the last monarch so to be. In spite of the poverty of the country, which was becoming acute and was compounded by outbreaks of plague, another Scots army was mustered at Stirling, and marched into England, with the king at its head, together with a number of Scots nobles and gentry. They marched deep into England by the west, but did not attract as much English support as they had hoped. Cromwell, who enjoyed a chase-about, caught up with them in the town of Worcester and had a total victory. Charles got away with difficulty to the Continent, and many Scots lords were imprisoned. These included Lauderdale and Tarbat, both future secretaries of state in the Restoration, and Sir Thomas Urquhart of Cromarty, scholar and eccentric, whose complaint that he had lost four portmanteaux of books and documents at Worcester got little sympathy—it was hardly practical to take research papers on campaign. Urquhart was paroled and went to France where he translated Rabelais into English more pungent, earthy and original than the French, proving, if proof were needed, that Highland gentlemen could be as scholarly and as bawdy as any in Europe.

After Worcester there was for a little no more organized opposition in Scotland, and Cromwell proceeded with some severity to settle both Ireland and Scotland. He offered each country a mere 30 members to attend the English Parliament, which was 400 members strong. He administered uncorrupt justice with a heavy hand through his nominees and his English army commanders. He was deeply disliked in Scotland, and his army was feared, and ignored when possible.

VI
Commonwealth and Restoration

Commonwealth and Cavaliers

DURING THE COMMONWEALTH period Scotland had a brief legal unity with England, during which first Colonel Lilburne and then General Monck ruled in the Lord Protector's name from headquarters at Dalkeith. The Protectorate was proclaimed in Scotland in May 1654. The army made admirable regulations, collected taxes with efficiency, and were a model of a military junta. But the Scots were ungrateful, disliked military rule and detested receiving their laws from Westminster. In the north a party of royalists expressed popular feeling by rising under Lord Glencairn. It was the first of the risings for the exiled house of Stewart (Charles II was in the Low Country at the time) and established a pattern which ran consistently and disastrously until Culloden, 90 years later. Glencairn had considerable initial success, and was joined by many of the great names in the north: Seaforth, Glengarry and Lochiel among them, and by a handful of Fife and Lowland gentry of whom Balcarres was a leader.

Charles II promised to send arms, artillery, men and gold from France, and sought to stop the inevitable rivalry by imposing his own choice of leader, General Middleton, a plausible and unsatisfactory soldier of fortune. Before Middleton could land—he was fruitlessly trying to collect the promised French reinforcements—Glencairn had tied up large numbers of the Commonwealth troops, had marched his guerrilla bands through Badenoch and Lennox, and sent forays into Lothian and Ayr, and even as far south as Carlisle. He received much passive support wherever he campaigned, and was often able to collect the cess (land tax) ahead of the government tax gatherers, from Scotsmen of good will who preferred to pay him rather than the English army. However, significant numbers hung back from joining the rising. Lilburne was faced with a crisis of loyalty, he had few troops and was short of money. He was replaced by Monck, who received reinforcements.

Monck in the North: 'rigor and ruyne'

Just as internal quarrels weakened the royalists Middleton landed at Tarbat in Easter Ross in 1653. His arrival did nothing to reconcile the ambitions of Glengarry, who hoped for an earldom from Charles II, nor the affront of the

superseded Glencairn, nor the ambitions of Balcarres. Seaforth's Mackenzies went off on a private punitive expedition against the MacLeods of Assynt whose territories would have made a pleasant addition to adjacent Mackenzie holdings and who had, by recently appearing to betray Montrose, made themselves a legitimate target. The Earl of Argyll stood staunch to the Commonwealth and English interest, but his son Lorne fought in Glencairn's force, and many lesser families similarly seem to have hedged their commitment.

Glencairn's rising, split on leadership issues, was desperately short of guns and gold, and did not receive adequate backing from the exiled king, neither did the French nor the Dutch fulfil any promises of aid. Monck marched in with his men sweating in their buff leather jackets and jackboots, going over some of the roughest territory north of the Great Glen. He hoped to prevent Lowland recruits and horses joining Middleton's force, and wrote to Cromwell that he was determined 'to pursue the rebels with rigor and ruyne'. He burnt all the standing crops and many townships, particularly in Kintail, Seaforth's domain. Monck's base was Cromwell's Citadel of Inverness, and a government galley patrolled Loch Ness. His men performed prodigies of marching as Middleton's forces split up and slipped away along the glens.

Eventually Monck began to take submissions from rebel leaders; Seaforth for one had to give a vast bond for good behaviour; however, he was allowed to keep his lands and repair his castle of Eilean Donan, and was given a commission to enforce the government's peace in Ross. Cess was remitted for two years because of the extent of destruction upon his lands. Cromwell's administration was faced by a continuing dilemma in the Highlands: law and order could only be enforced with the cooperation of the great men of the north. The document which Seaforth signed with Monck in Inverness reads more like a treaty between princes than the submission of a rebel subject.

Cromwell died in 1658 and Monck went south, eventually to cross the Channel and bring back King Charles II to London. The bells pealed in Edinburgh, and the Restoration was proclaimed at the Mercat Cross by Lyon King of Arms.

Immediately a great jostling for place and royal favour broke out, and a certain amount of embarrassment was felt by warm supporters of presbytery and parliamentary rule. There were a number of practical difficulties. In spite of the enhanced political sophistication of the Scots people, and their experience of independent presbyterian government, the clock was put back to the earlier pattern of James VI, that of an independent kingdom ruled remotely by the king in London through his great officers of state and the Privy Council of Scotland. A Restoration Parliament was called and throughout most of the reign the Scots Parliament worked hard and often constructively.

The chief question was, did all those well-respected men who had served Parliament and the Commonwealth have to retire from public life, and was all the legislation of the war years to be wiped out? Before compromises could be reached an attempt was made by the 'furious Cavaliers' of the extreme royalist party to exclude, by ballot, the Puritans from office. This measure was defeated by Lauderdale who though a Presbyterian had already won the royal favour and was Secretary of State. Lauderdale managed to dislodge Middleton, the Cavaliers' leader, from power. Middleton, as King's Commissioner and governor of Edinburgh Castle, had overseen the execution of that Earl of Argyll who had shown such zeal for the Commonwealth. Middleton was dismissed, to become Governor of Tangier, where he took to the bottle. Lauderdale ran Scotland for the king, with some competence, for the next 17 years. One of the first official acts of the Restoration in Scotland was to have the poor scattered bones of Montrose collected from the bow gates of the cities where they had been exposed, and to stage an ornate state funeral.

Restoration Scotland was full of hope for a new and peaceful régime, with new beginnings in science and learning; with latitude in worship, which enabled men to take their own paths to some unaccustomed degree, and with a return to the laws of Scotland, it was a time of recurring nostalgia and hope for the future. The law was stimulated in several ways, and its prestige enhanced by the formation of the Court of Judiciary in 1677 to hear criminal cases, and by the attempt by Mackenzie of Rosehaugh to codify the laws of Scotland in his *Institutions*; a few years later Lord Stair produced his weightier *Institutions*:

Sir William Bruce rebuilt the palace of Holyroodhouse

Mackenzie of Tarbat began the systematic retention of civil documents in a Register during his term as Clerk Register. The Faculty of Advocates laid down professional qualifications and opened their library, and the physicians of Edinburgh banded together in 1682, in the face of opposition from the surgeon-apothecaries, and formed the Royal College of Physicians in Edinburgh (Glasgow had been ahead of them).

For all this intellectual activity, the land was fettered and frustrated by poverty. Taxation was through the levying of the cess. The assessment for the land tax had been made so long ago that its collection worked to the benefit of landowners, whose lands had much increased in value though the cess had not, thus the cess had become a far from adequate source of national income. The Customs and Excise dues and the dues from the royal burghs were also collected by rather haphazard means, and many astute landowners began to obtain charters to turn convenient villages or harbours on their land into burghs of barony, which undercut the official royal burghs, thus attracting trade but putting the profits into baronial pockets, and causing great hardship to the royal burghs. Their Convention is full of laments about 'ports much decayit' while newer towns flourished, without paying so many taxes. Such dues as the crown did succeed in raising were often paid into the Treasury greatly in arrears, and as a result the office bearers of the crown were also paid in arrears. A scramble to multiply the holding of offices, and much corruption, were partly consequences of the erratic arrival of the 'fruits of office' as regular pay.

Economic difficulties

Efforts to 'increase the wealth of the realm', in the phrase of the day, often took the form of obtaining a royal monopoly through Parliament for the manufacture or sale of some commodity, such as soap or paper. The lack of capital and of expertise almost invariably caused these attempts to fail quite quickly. The worst handicap that the Scots suffered in their attempts to increase the wealth of the realm was imposed by the English Navigation Law. From the time of James VI's arrival in England, English merchants had received the backing of Parliament to exclude Scots from trade across the Atlantic. From Cromwell's day onwards these laws were strengthened, aimed primarily at the Dutch, but adversely affecting the Scots too.

A long look at the kirk

The complicated and sometimes tedious accounts of the religious struggles of the seventeenth century should not blind us to the real human dilemmas which men faced, as they honestly tried to decide between God and the state. Echoes of that time of trial still have power to move us. The high-church demands of Charles I had evoked strong resistance throughout Scotland, producing first the National Covenant and secondly the General Assembly of Glasgow in 1638. This was the first time an Assembly had asserted its claim to have supreme authority over the church, and (by implication) over the state too. This principle had been formulated by the *Second Book of Discipline* of 1578, and subsequently been included in the presbyterian teaching of Andrew Melville. The claim had not been pressed. The crown increasingly supported bishops and considered they acted as a political brake on independence, and were integral to the kirk. By 1638 church affairs had become passionately polarized. The Glasgow Assembly, possibly 'packed', attacked the bishops as a symbol of royal control, with every verbal weapon at their command, denying them any place in the kirk. It was a revolution and it left a deep mark on the Scottish national consciousness. Acknowledgement of bishops, liturgy and the episcopal ordering of the kirk became popularly equated in the Lowlands with unpatriotic, alien and English practices. In the north, however, an episcopal kirk was still desired.

As the civil wars fluctuated, and especially after Cromwell at Dunbar had inflicted a very marked and chastening defeat on the Covenanting army, public opinion began to swing away from extreme theocracy towards support of the monarchy. When in 1660 the king was restored the general hope in Scotland was for a moderate form of presbyterian settlement, and the fear was that the excesses of the extreme Covenanting party might have alienated Charles II. An active minister, James Sharp, was sent to London to persuade the administration to grant presbyterian status to the Scottish church. He conferred with Lauderdale and other influential Scots nobles, who were of like mind. However Argyll, also in London, was arrested and sent back to Scotland, where he was executed for his strong support of the Covenant, as was Guthrie, minister of Stirling. This diminished support (as was intended) for more militant forms of presbyterianism. Sharp, however, reported back encouragingly to his supporters in Edinburgh on the chances of a moderate presbyterian settlement.

Charles II's first Scottish Parliament early in 1661, however, was required to pass a number of royal Acts forbidding further Covenanting, rescinding all legislation back to 1633 and establishing that the king would maintain his supremacy over the church, and that its doctrine and worship would be that as 'established within this Kingdome dureing the reigne of his royall father and grandfather'. Kirk sessions, presbyteries and synods were permitted to be held, though any private prayer meeting or 'conventicle' was strictly forbidden. Synods in Fife, Galloway, Dumfries and Glasgow promptly met and rejected the implied reintroduction of bishops: as promptly they were dissolved by royal proclamation. By the end of the year further legislation had confirmed the reintroduction of bishops and Sharp returned from London with royal appointment as Archbishop Sharp of St Andrews, for which he forfeited much esteem. Other bishops were also appointed.

An Oath of Allegiance to the King, entailing recognition of his overall spiritual authority, was enacted in 1663, and proved unpalatable but acceptable to most, but not to a minority in the south-west. Nonconforming ministers and preachers, who had not taken the Oath, began to hold open-air conventicles, as they were denied the use of kirks. The conventiclers, in fear of arrest, began using arms and gradually took on a militant character. In 1666 a small government force was sent to police the south-west, under Thomas Dalyell of the Binns with Sir James Turner and Sir William Drummond as lieutenants. They collected punitive fines in Ayr and Galloway, then Turner's provocative behaviour turned a scuffle at Dalry into

an armed insurrection which soon ended in pitched battle at Rullion Green, in the Pentland Hills. Dalyell took 80 prisoners, and many others were hunted through the south-west. Some were hanged, others transported to the West Indies. At the end of 1667 Dalyell was discredited and his army disbanded; conciliation was then the policy of the day.

Conciliation as practised by Bishop Leighton of Glasgow was not successful and conventicling—private and illicit devotions—was widespread. After 1669 it was apparently strongest in Fife and on the east coast. The adherents of the Established Kirk were at a disadvantage, conformity was not dramatic.

Years of harassment by the government, and of lawlessness by conventiclers, came to a head again in 1677. The government dispatched Highland troops to free-quarter, and to patrol in south-west Scotland. The murder of Archbishop Sharp in Fife added to tensions. Armed insurrection again followed. The conventiclers, among whom Richard Cameron was the most radical and vocal, took up arms. The government sent a large detachment to reduce them, commanded by the Duke of Monmouth, with Graham of Claverhouse as his lieutenant; they brought a pitched battle to victory at Bothwell Brig. The numbers involved were small, but the emotions were strong on either side. Most of the Scots were for a peaceable life, in the Lowlands men were of a presbyterian habit, and in the Highlands of a more episcopalian tinge. Only retrospectively did the conventiclers and the 'Cameronians' take on a heroic aspect as defenders of presbyterian beliefs, and their political intentions seem less important than they appeared to contemporaries.

Charles II sent his brother and heir, James Duke of York, to Scotland at a point towards the end of his reign when James's open enthusiasm for the Roman Church had caused such alarm in England that he had barely escaped an Act of Exclusion from the succession. It might be thought that to send him to Scotland in such circumstances was to ask for trouble, but curiously he was made welcome in the capital. It was a long time since a court had been held at Holyroodhouse, though Charles II had ordered the old palace to be rebuilt and refurbished by Sir William Bruce, work just completed in 1678 before James Duke of York arrived, with his younger Protestant daughter Anne, and his second Catholic wife Mary of Modena. They spent at least two periods of semi-exile in Edinburgh, confirming good relations with a number of the court party of nobles, opening the Scots Parliament which had not met for some years previously, proposing the revival of the old Stewart Order of the Thistle (on Catholic lines) and generally shocking and intriguing the citizens of the capital. Catholic priests and Restoration frolics were something new in Edinburgh. Playacting and the drinking of those new temptations, tea and coffee, and the planting of tulips and narcissi from Holland in the cold gardens of the Lothians, can be laid at the door of the Duke of York and his court. The irreverent students of Edinburgh University, however, burnt an effigy of the Pope in the Canongate; the court was a welcome spectacle in drab times, but no example to follow.

King James VII

VII

James VII and II

The White Rose and the House of Orange

JAMES VII AND II when he came to the throne showed overt enthusiasm for the Catholic faith, and sought to endear himself and to bring acceptance for it by Acts of Tolerance which also gave latitude for worship to Quakers, English Presbyterians and other banned nonconformist sects. This naturally disturbed the orthodox Presbyterians, and few wanted Rome restored in Scotland. However, the court party had a number of fellow travellers and some of the nobility saw fit to become converts, thus to advance their prospects in this world. A few of course had not ceased to be Catholic. Among James's strongest supporters was John Graham of Claverhouse, a soldier who had commanded the government forces which put down the covenanting revolt of 1678 with harshness. He did well out of loyalty to James, who made him Constable of Dundee and First Magistrate, which gave black affront to the Provost and burgesses of that town. In 1688 he was declared Provost by royal Act.

Most of the gentry of Scotland had been mildly episcopalian since the restoration: James forced his Catholic belief and his belief in the divine right of kings onto increasingly reluctant subjects in both kingdoms. He brought over Irish troops to back up his authority. Mary of Modena, his second wife, eventually produced a son and heir in London, James, born on 10 June 1688. The day was honoured as White Rose Day by Jacobites for the next 100 years. The birth of a Catholic heir was the last straw in English eyes—the nobles of England had not had the long experience of royal minorities which the Scots had enjoyed and the English failed to see that legitimacy could have been maintained and the Protestant succession assured by the simple device of detaching the royal infant from his parents and bringing him up a Protestant, as had been done with James VI. The taverns of London sang a new ditty:

> Rock-a-bye baby . . .
> When the bough breaks . . .

Queen Mary fled to France with the infant as the capital prepared to welcome Dutch William: James followed, returned, dithered, and was quietly sent off again from Dover. No one was quite sure if he had abdicated or retreated—did he jump or was he pushed? At any rate his rule was forfeited and his impeccably Protestant son-in-law, married to his elder Protestant daughter Mary, came over the Channel to general Whig rejoicing in England. He brought 14,000 Dutch troops with him, to ensure a welcome. Everyone whistled and sang 'Lillibullero', a catchy tune said to have 'whistled a King out of three Kingdoms'. James attempted a counter-attack through Ireland and mustered a large army stiffened by French, but was routed at the battle of the Boyne. 'King Billy', William of Orange, the victor, became a folk hero to the anti-Papist Scotsmen and Ulstermen, though the formation of the Orange Order as a formal expression of their sentiments did not occur until the end of the eighteenth century, and was among the political schemes of Ernest Duke of Cumberland.

The Scots felt far more ambivalent than did the English at James's going. While his beliefs and politics were generally detested, there was far more loyalty to the old house of Stewart, which had ruled the northern kingdom for three centuries. The Parliament of Scotland, or (in the absence of a crowned head to call it) the Convention of Estates, met in Edinburgh to consider the Scottish position. Before it were two letters. William of Orange promised nothing but a strict adherence to the Protestant faith, James wrote a snarl of royal absolutism, demanding obedience, reiterating divine right, and conceding nothing. The Scots voted solidly for William, and shuffled the pack again, hoping for places at the new court. The small number of dissidents began calling themselves Jacobites, after the absent king, but only John Graham of Claverhouse took an army into the field in his name, recruited from the Catholic Highlands in the main. He had gained no support in the capital. Graham won an immortal name by being slain in the hour of victory at Killiecrankie where a Highland charge had won a seemingly impossible victory. A month later his fragmented force was defeated at Dunkeld in a small battle where the government's commander, Colonel Cleland, was also slain in the hour of victory—but he was an upright Covenanter of no personal charm: no one called him Bonny nor made ballads about the affair, as they did about Dundee. Peace settled uneasily on Scotland, but little further was heard about the Jacobites for some time.

Prince James Edward Stuart,
the 'rock-a-bye baby'

James VII and II

Distress and oath taking

It was peace and years of pinched economy and, in the Lothians and Central Scotland, outright famine. Three years of bad harvest and bad weather had ruined grain stocks, the seed corn was eaten, hunger and disease carried off hundreds. The plague reappeared; there was dire distress. Transport was too rudimentary to enable aid to be brought from the less affected areas such as Moray. Round the Moray Firth distress took a more political form. Because of the known disaffection and suspected treasonable activities of such magnates as Lovat the government sent troops to be quartered on the households of Inverness

William of Orange

and Ross, and imposed heavy levies for food and fodder. Rumour ran fast and inaccurately round the counties. The territorial magnates still held commissions of the peace, and less officially ran their own lands. Politically the country was in the doldrums.

Half the inhabitants of Scotland still lived 'benorth the Forth' and that territory fell roughly into quarters, dominated by magnates with different approaches to the topics of the day, though with a uniform appetite for power and land. Huntly and the Catholic Gordon connection were dominant in the north-east; further north and west, power was tightly held in Mackenzie hands—episcopalian with a hereditary loyalty to the house of Stewart tempered by highly practical considerations. The Mackenzies' handicap was to be led by successive earls of Seaforth, volatile, Catholic and spendthrift of their followers' lands and lives. Only the prudent legalistic approaches of the two George Mackenzies, Rosehaugh and Tarbat, preserved the Mackenzie hegemony for another generation. Further north in Sutherland the staunchly Protestant Mackays provided a succession of soldiers and government servants both to the crown and to the United Provinces. Eventually their territories were eroded by Gordons, as happened to the northernmost magnates, the Sinclairs, who had trouble with encroaching Campbells. Atholl, with lands leading to the Highland passes, was uncommitted in affairs of church and state; succeeding earls of Atholl perched on the fence with the practice born of years. In the Islands and mainland of the west the vacuum caused by the fall of the MacDonald lords of the Isles had been filled by lesser families, and by the steady advance of the house of Argyll, which was consolidating 100 years of gains. Royal trust and reliance on Argyll to police the west had increased Campbell power, reinforcing their firm commitment to presbyterian principles and, later, to Whig political sentiment. Two earls suffered execution for their principles, the Eighth, after the Restoration, for his support of Cromwell, and the Ninth for his abortive rising in the west in support of Monmouth's Protestant rising against James VII in 1685. These losses did not affect the steady aggrandizement of the clan, nor the overall ability of its members.

The MacDonalds of Glencoe

King William turned out to be almost wholly uninterested in Scottish affairs, and inclined to leave decisions to his private secretary Carstairs, a Scot and an extreme Presbyterian who had come with him from Holland. William regarded Scotland only as a good source of recruits for his army and a poor source of finance. His main interest remained foreign affairs and his interminable wars, based on the Low Countries against Catholic kings. He departed each spring on campaign, leaving the vaguest instructions about his northern kingdom in the hands of the Secretary of State, Stair, and other officers of the realm who had to rule in the king's name (and keep his favour) and to protect their own interests from the intrigues of their compeers. William, with Carstairs at his elbow,

Argyll

abolished the 1669 Act of Supremacy, and confirmed presbyterian order in the kirk. The bishops and many ministers were 'outed'.

The loyalty of the northern chiefs was still in doubt and had to be secured by their taking an oath of allegiance to King William and the Protestant settlement. Some honourably awaited King James's letter of release from their former allegiance, which eventually came. In 1690 Mackenzie of Tarbat was engaged by the king, as a useful all-purpose statesman with a wide knowledge of the chiefs and their kinships and their current states of indebtedness, to secure peace in the Highlands. Tarbat saw clearly that what worried most landowners in the west of Scotland was the encroachment of the Campbells of Argyll on their land, much of which was in dispute. He proposed that the crown bought up the disputed superiorities and compensated the aggrieved parties, and this was accepted with alacrity by some. Lochiel honestly professed his relief. In close alliance with old Colonel Hill, veteran of Monck's campaign in the north, who commanded the army, Tarbat was fairly successful in buying the superiorities and persuading the chiefs to take the oath. Hill rebuilt the old Cromwellian fortress of Inverlochy which was named Fort William, in compliment. Tarbat, however, was displaced by Argyll through intrigues in Kensington Palace in favour of Campbell nominees. Tarbat himself was replaced by Campbell of Breadalbane, who was in his own words 'an old fox holed up in the hills'.

Nearly all the chiefs had taken the oath by 1 January 1692, the due day, but a few were late, including the aged head of the small group of McIan MacDonalds of Glencoe, who arrived on 6 January. McIan's fault was given a quite usual punishment; troops were sent to Glen Coe and stationed at free-quarter on the clan. This meant that the inhabitants had to find food for them and their horses, and firing. This was quite a burden on small communities with few reserves, and one which was justifiably resented all over the Highlands. It was at this time that troops at free-quarter were deployed all over Easter Ross and Inverness-shire watching for signs of revolt, and bitterly disliked. But only in Glen Coe did the troops act, under orders, with outright barbarity. They turned on their hosts and killed 38 out of the clan of about a hundred and fifty. The Campbell regiment concerned was not particularly efficient, or perhaps some connived in the escape through high passes of many of the clan.

As the long early history of massacres in the Highlands went, it was not a particularly bloody affair, but public opinion was outraged by the illegality of the proceedings, and the implicit assumption that ordinary laws did not apply to the Highlands. A parliamentary inquiry was demanded, but sidetracked in 1693 (and Breadalbane got the grazing). Two years later a second inquiry condemned the government for having 'barbarously killed men under trust'. The real threat to peace in the north was that Campbell aggression and land hunger, far from being checked, had been given a legal veneer, and confidence in the Williamite administration had declined.

'*A*' the dreary years'

To daunton me, to daunton me
Do you ken the thing that would daunton me?
Eighty-eight and eighty-nine
An a' the dreary years since syne,
With Cess and Press and Presbytry
Good Faith, this had liken till a' daunton me.

But to wanton me, but to wanton me,
And ken ye what maist would wanton me?
To see King James at Edinburgh Cross,
With fifty thousand foot and horse,
And the Usurper forced to flee—
O this is what maist would wanton me![1]

Anon, *circa* 1694

Popular opinion was inclined to attribute all the ills of King William's reign to the change of ruler. King William, who never visited his 'Ancient Kingdom', had a much more pragmatic attitude towards it than had the Stewart kings, who had 'married' the kingdom in the old coronation rites at Scone. The politicians and

[1] The thing that most daunts me is 1688, 1689 and all the dreary years since, with land cess tax, military impressments and rigid ministers . . . but the thing that most would cheer me up is to see King James in Edinburgh with a big force of men, and the end of 'King' William . . .

the merchants and ministers of Scotland were much too sophisticated to think along those lines, but the people had a stubborn regard for the old days when things had seemed better, and connected present distress with the change on the throne. However, many, from all walks of life, were inclined to blame most of the ills of the country onto the English. Whatever the cause, there was severe economic distress, leading to some instability.

The efforts of the merchants and lairds to increase commerce were handicapped by local famines and food shortages, and the Navigation Laws of England. A few of the enterprising men of Glasgow and the west of Scotland established bases in Whitehaven, across the Solway on English soil, from which to send merchantmen across the Atlantic; Newcastle also held a large Scottish colony mostly engaged on the Baltic trade. Much money was ventured at home, and mostly it was lost on schemes to manufacture such consumer-desirables as green glass bottles, linen, paper, or playing cards in Scotland. Complaints were made in the Scots Parliament that these ventures failed because the English undercut prices, dumped excessive amounts of cheap goods, and when the infant Scottish industries buckled and failed, the English then raised the prices of their imports. It was a sour and mutually hostile relationship. The Dutch too were better at fishing Scottish waters and brought their busses (factory ships) insolently close inshore to take the good Scots herrings.

Scotland was short of capital and of good management, and the internal markets were too small to stimulate manufacture. The gentry however increasingly raised their demand for consumer goods and minor luxuries, and the building of a country seat in place of the old fortified tower became almost a necessity in polite society. In William's reign the first Act for the encouragement of land enclosure forecast future evictions, 'improvement', and the relentless pressure by landowners to increase their rentals and the output of their land. Already some were growing turnips and potatoes, though these were still only

planted in walled gardens, and were considered luxuries. Other enterprising men were attempting to improve the breeds of cattle, sheep and horses by importing new strains. As yet these efforts showed results as meagre as the first industries.

The Scots found their small but ancient trades with France and the Low Countries and the Baltic all involved with the international complications of English foreign policy. The worst hindrance to trade was caused by the English Navigation Laws, passed by degrees through the preceding generation. In an age given to mercantilist theories each country jealously guarded its own stocks of bullion, and feared that competition would diminish their share of the world's absolute wealth. The English, who had started in rivalry with the Dutch, particularly feared the competition of the more thrifty and perhaps hungry Scots, and the Navigation Laws were framed therefore to exclude the Scots as well as the Dutch entirely from any share in colonial trade, either to the Americas, or to India where the monopoly of the Honourable East India Company ran from the Cape of Good Hope to the China Seas. No foreign ships could trade with English colonies or factories overseas, and no goods could be shipped in or out except in English vessels. It was a total exclusion. France too began erecting tariff barriers

and the Baltic trade also diminished; Scots trade was in a dire depression, and the famines of the 'ill years' had taken internal toll.

In an effort to break out and to take part in the lucrative colonial trade it was proposed that the Scots should set up their own monopoly: 'The Company of Scotland Trading to Africa and the Indies'. The initiative came from London, from rivals to the tight circle of East India merchants there, but the idea was enthusiastically taken up in Scotland. A subscription list was opened in 1695 and Scots vied to find the capital to invest in the company. Then the magnates of the London East India Company took action to ward off the interlopers, threatening the English directors of the Scottish company with impeachment in Parliament and drying up (through diplomatic pressures) the possible overseas sources of capital, particularly in Hamburg. The English government supported the East India Company; no help for the Scots was forthcoming. The Scots were forced to raise the money alone and to manage the enterprises without any experience of either colonial trade or large-scale investment of this nature.

One small venture to Africa did reasonably well, one to Madagascar ended in piracy and disaster, but the venture to America was total disaster. Management in Edinburgh had been taken over by a plausible Scot, William Paterson, who advocated the little-known Darien peninsula on the west coast of Panama as an ideal site to found a colony and an entrepôt that would handle the trade of both the Caribbean and of the Pacific. The prospectus he drew up was glowing, and people put their savings and their daughters' dowries into his company. The ships sailed for Darien in two expeditions. The site for Fort St Andrew was a fever-ridden swamp, in territory claimed by the King of Spain and inhabited by a handful of Amerindians. Spain at this point was an ally of England, and this intensified Spanish indignation at the Scottish settlement. Ships of the English Navy harassed the Scottish fleet, and the English Governor of Jamaica refused assistance. The goods that Scotland had to trade with were pathetically unsuitable: such things as blue woollen Kilmarnock bonnets and quires of thick wrapping paper had no sale. There was in any case no one to trade with. In all, the Scots lost the lives of many men, and over five years the money lost was £150,000 sterling or £1.8M Scots, astronomical for an impoverished country. The Darien Venture, courageously undertaken, was a complete disaster. Anger was concentrated on the English, though some should have been directed at Paterson and the inept handling of the affair. The high feelings and the loss coloured all the Scottish attitudes to England.

Queen Anne holding court

VIII

The Union and after

WILLIAM OF ORANGE died in 1702 quite unlamented by his Scottish subjects. They indeed called his reign 'King William's Ill Years' and were ominously beginning to quote Scripture about the 'Right of the First-born Son'. This was rank treason, going clean against the Revolutionary Settlement of 1688, since it put forward the claim of James Francis Edward, son of James VII (who also died in 1702). The exiled king had held his court at St Germain as a pensioner of the King of France, and at his death his son James Edward was acknowledged by the French king as 'James III of England and VIII of Scotland'. The French saw in the exiled Jacobite court an excellent potential source of dissension and weakness in Britain. James Edward continued for the present to live at St Germain with his mother and a small band of convinced and penurious Jacobite adherents. A larger number of passing English and Scottish gentry visited them out of loyalty, curiosity or a prudent desire not to be found wholly out of sympathy with the 'king over the water' in case of a restoration. Whiggish elements called James Francis Edward the 'Pretender'; his least controversial title was 'Chevalier de St Georges'.

Queen Anne, sister of Mary and half-sister of James Edward, came to the throne in 1702. Throughout her reign the Jacobite court in exile presented a threat, a possible alternative to her and her successor. There were many covert Jacobite sympathizers and a few active plotters, identified in England with the nickname Tory, and with the Anglican high-church party. This situation was obviously dangerous for the security of the countries, a danger intensified by the outbreak of war between France and England. The War of the Spanish Succession which began in 1703 was the first of the long wars for colonial supremacy which occupied the European powers for the eighteenth century.

It was becoming increasingly clear that Scottish independence in economic terms was dwindling to nothing in the shadow of the dominant partner. The Scots Parliament struggled to maintain its independent status, but this was particularly difficult in the field of foreign affairs. When England went to war the Scots were angered to learn that their kingdom too had been committed, and were stubborn when required to put a ban on the import of French wines, and on the export of woollen goods. They passed two Acts to encourage just these two activities. Scotsmen had always preferred claret, whereas the ban did not affect the English much; their wine trade was with their old ally, Portugal. Nor did the Scottish woollen trade benefit much from defiance, as the wily English merchants sent their broadcloth north to be exported from Scottish ports, outselling the inferior home product. Then an issue of larger dimensions came up: the Scots at last obtained some leverage through the question of the succession to Queen Anne. The poor queen's 17 pregnancies had not resulted in one surviving child. The English and Whig candidate for the succession was the elderly Electress Sophie of Hanover, and her son George. He was one of the many great-grandchildren of James VI and I, a German princeling who was a good military man and a reliable Protestant, a suitable choice in the eyes of many.

The Scots were disenchanted by distant monarchy. Since 1651 when Charles II had been more or less a prisoner of the Covenanters, no monarch had crossed the border to affirm a Scottish identity or to acknowledge his Scottish subjects. The Scots pound was a deplorable one-twelfth of a pound sterling in value; colonial trade was illegal by English law and therefore clandestine and difficult; trade with France was hampered not only by English attempts to discourage it but also by increasing French tariff barriers. Coal and fish still went to the Low Countries, but not in qualities great enough to balance the imports of Scotland.

With these difficulties, the Scots Parliament proposed a radical solution to the succession, putting forward an Act of Security. In effect this was a veiled proposal for a return to total independence, for the first draft of the Act proposed that the next monarch of Scotland should be anyone but George, Elector of Hanover, providing he was a Protestant and of legitimate Stewart blood. There were nearly fifty Stewart kin abroad in Europe at this time: the first in legitimacy, however, was the Chevalier, James Edward, and he was a resolute Catholic. In an echo of earlier sentiments the proposed Act of Security opted for 'such conditions of government settled and enacted as may secure the honour and independence of the crown of this kingdom'. At the same time the Scots Parliament withheld the vote on Supply (the transference of taxation to the Treasury). The English government was forced to take notice of this defiance, particularly as Marlborough's campaign against the French was at its height. No government in time of war could afford so much unrest in a neighbouring partner. It became generally recognized that the status of both countries had to be re-examined.

Negotiations were opened again for a union of parliaments. It was a matter which had been discussed in a desultory way ever since Cromwell's Commonwealth union, but nothing had ever come of it. It took some time to start the discussions, and the Scots succeeded in bringing English attention to themselves (and creating in England the same boiling indignation that the Scots had so often felt). They hanged an English sea captain caught in Leith and thought, on little evidence, to have contributed to the Darien disaster. On the English side there seems to have been a lack of interest and urgency over union. The Scots too were deeply divided in their attitudes. Those who advocated union were the parliamentarians and lords whose interests were most closely involved with the politics and economy of the country and who saw the material benefits of union. Many of the large landowners had interests in cattle droving which was the biggest export, and most had connections with such manufacturing industry as existed; in the west improvement of trade with the colonies was seen as crucial to Scotland. Opposed to union, the citizens of most burghs feared competition and terms of parity with England, and the Jacobites looked for a return to the past, and independence. The extreme kirk party were against union from another angle, fearing a threat to the Established Church of Scotland. Queensberry, the Queen's Commissioner for Scotland, had great problems in negotiating the terms during the long and public debate in Parliament in Edinburgh. A pamphlet war raged and public opinion was deeply divided.

The Treaty of Union was finally passed by the Scots Parliament, who last met on 28 April 1707. It was, in the words of Chancellor Seafield, 'ane end of ane auld sang'. The Treaty of Union became law in May 1707.

The terms of union

In spite of the high passions of the day, and the varied criticisms of later generations, it is possible to think that the terms of union were on the whole reasonable. Key institutions were retained in Scotland, including the whole apparatus of Scots law and the courts of the land. The kirk was secured as the Established Church of Scotland, by separate legislation, and the educational system was left intact. These three institutions, law, kirk and college, gave continuity and identity to national life.

On the political side, the Scots acknowledged the future succession of the House of Hanover, and the two parliaments were merged into one of the United Kingdom of Great Britain. The new assembly was to meet at Westminster, and naturally the customs of the larger and more mature House of Commons were carried on without a break: only 45 Scottish members joined the 513 Westminster MPs. Sixteen 'representative peers' were elected by the Scottish peerage to sit in the House of Lords. At a time when wealth and 'interest' were considered more important than numerical representation of the people this was a fair reflection of the relative wealths of England and Scotland. The Scots peerage became a closed circle and the retention of the court of arbitration presided over by the Lyon King at Arms kept the Scots peerage's continuity. The refusal of the government to recognize the right of all Scots peers to sit in the House of Lords rankled deeply, especially with those who held in addition an English title that would have given them a seat if their primary title had not been Scots. These politically ambitious peers included the Duke of Hamilton and Brandon and the Duke of Argyll and Greenwich, two of the most powerful men in Scotland; their hostility made it a far from trivial issue.

More important, however, were the economic provisions of the Treaty. The Navigation Laws were extended to include Scotland, opening the colonies to Scottish trade and the employment of Scottish talent. Customs and Excise regulations covering the whole of Great Britain made it the biggest single free-trading area in Europe, a factor in the rapid industrial growth of the next 100 years. Taxes on malt and salt, along English lines, were deferred in Scotland for a few years because of their great unpopularity; they bore hardest on the poor and struck at essentials. The financial arrangements were of the greatest importance. The English government had a more formal and advanced system of national accounting than the Scots had, and desired that Scotland assume a share of the newly set up National Debt. Scotland too was in debt, but this was unacknowledged by the haphazard methods of the Scots Treasury. The depreciated Scots currency, the empty exchequer and the great arrears of salary payment to government servants were more obvious. Pay to all, including the highest in the land, was about seven years in arrears and not any number of new titles and advancement could take the place of cash due. The solution was for England to clear the slate, sending north two waggonloads of specie to equalize the National Debt and pay the arrears and some of the Darien losses. Those government servants who could make good claims got their arrears, and as these were largely the same men who negotiated the union, charges of bribery and corruption were inevitable. It is difficult to judge the truth; interestingly the charges were made more strongly later, when the defects of union had become more noticeable than the advantages. Two generations later Robert Burns, that great patriot, wrote:

> They were bought and sold for English gold
> Such a parcel of Rogues in a Nation.

The Scots politicians of the day were not great men, but not despicable either. They were impoverished and saw the country growing poorer; they fought quite successfully for a share with a stronger partner, partly for personal ends but mainly for the good of the country as they saw it. And whatever was extinguished by the Treaty of Union, it was not the Scottish identity of character.

After union: 'The Fifteen'

The euphoria induced by union was short lived. The enthusiasts like old Lord Tarbat could write, 'Now there is no more England or Scotland, but one Great Britain,' but somehow neither the English nor the Scots ever caught the verbal habit. Today Queen Anne's successor at nine removes is still more often called Queen of England than Queen of the United Kingdom of Great Britain. The English were simply not very interested in Scotland though there was a slighting habit of referring to it as 'N B'—North Britain.

English officers arrived to reform the corrupt and chaotic old Scots Customs and Excise. They efficiently imposed an even more complicated system and planned to tax malt, as in England. This threatened to raise the price of fundamental needs, beer and whisky. The malt tax was deferred but its eventual imposition caused the worst urban riots that Scotland had ever seen. In other ways the economic benefits of union were slow to mature and little immediate advantage was seen. The droving trade improved; it was no longer necessary to smuggle herds past border checkpoints. The sale of cattle and sheep on the hoof to England became a mainstay of Scotland's economy and paid the landlords' rents. Glasgow's rise as a colonial entrepôt gathered momentum. Still, the mood of the country in the years immediately after union was one of disaffection and disillusion.

Seven years after union Queen Anne died and ended hopes that she would nominate her half-brother, the Chevalier James Edward, as her heir. The Whigs of England had the Elector of Hanover waiting. George I had little personal charm: most could admire the abstract principles of legitimacy, the Protestant succession and parliamentary government for which he stood, but few could honestly admire the man. He spoke only German, his court was stiffly military and Germanic and his official mistresses were, to British eyes, of such stunning ugliness as to give rise to speculation and much ribaldry. Nevertheless, the nobility of both realms found it prudent to pay court. At a formal presentation at

Greenwich George I chose to ignore the bow of John Earl of Mar even though he was a former Secretary of State for Scotland. Mar, whose obsequious and time-serving manner had got him the by-name of 'Bobbing John', took umbrage, returned to Scotland and organized a shooting party. The stag drives of the Braes of Mar had long been famous sporting occasions, and most of the active nobility came. While the deer were being driven in they discussed the affairs of the nation. A few weeks later Mar raised the white standard of the House of Stewart and the Jacobite rising of 1715 had begun, with Mar, Seaforth, Sinclair, Huntly and MacIntosh of Borlum at its head. They all held lands in the north-east and the Highlands. Mar, for one, appears to have seen that his tenantry were forced out into his army.

At first there was a good deal of tacit support; both the union and George I, the 'wee German lairdie', were unpopular. A last throw for Scottish independence, even under the known hazards of a Catholic Stewart, was attractive. But Mar was no leader, and bungled his military dispositions, loitering with his army at Perth and disputing the leadership in classic Jacobite style. The most able soldier in his force, MacIntosh of Borlum, led a small party south to join up with the English Catholics of Northumbria and Lancashire. Mar's delays gave Argyll time to muster adequate forces for King George's government. Argyll, 'Red John of the Battles', was an able soldier who had served on Marlborough's staff with distinction. He must also have been a skilled propagandist; by successfully claiming victory at the inconclusive battle of Sherriffmuir in November 1715 Argyll secured the Hanoverian succession for Great Britain and almost entirely eclipsed the hopes of the Jacobites. The Chevalier James Edward, with his usual lack of good timing, landed at Peterhead too late to take part in the battle but in time to be associated with the infamous Jacobite order to burn to the ground the small Perthshire towns of Blackford and Auchterarder. MacIntosh of Borlum and the English Jacobites surrendered at Preston in Lancashire; James Edward returned to exile.

The rising of 1715 gave birth to far more robust balladry than the '45 did. The latter produced drawing-room songs, long after the event, while the '15 produced rough immediate verse. 'Cam' ye o'er frae France?' is one; the last verse goes (to a swinging weavers' rhythm) like this:

> Hey for Sandy Don[1]
> Hey for Cockalorum[2]
> Hey for Bobbing John[3]
> And his Highland quorum!
> Mony a sword and lance
> Swings at Highland hurdie[4]
> —How they'll skip and dance
> O'er the bum o' Geordie!

[1] ? The Earl of Seaforth [2] Huntly, Cock of the North [3] The Earl of Mar [4] bare buttocks

Burns, long after, collected a long ballad about 'The Sherramoor' which fairly accurately charts the course of the fight. In another the plight of the frightened English commander of dragoons is described too graphically for polite quotation. Not all the remaining songs are for King Jamie, though Jacobite songs tend to be better light verse than the Whiggish ones which went in for parody and heavy irony. New words were set in a mood of deepest satire to the Whig theme song 'Lillibullero'.

A Protestant Church from Rome doth advance . . .
And what is more rare, brings freedom, from France . . .

IX

The early Eighteenth Century

Acting in the king's interest

IN SPITE OF many Jacobite risings in the early eighteenth century the politics of Scotland were then perhaps the least interesting feature of national life. A series of able managers mediated Scottish affairs for the government in London. The government's aim was always to produce a safe and uncontroversial majority of Scottish M Ps who would support their measures without tedious argument. The franchise was very small, and the 30 shire seats could be swung by bribery, threats of violence or the more subtle pressure exerted by the landowner. The manufacture of fictitious votes became a fine art. The royal burghs had been allocated 15 seats and were joined in 'districts of burghs'. Glasgow for example was banded with Rutherglen, Dumbarton, and Renfrew. Edinburgh alone returned its own Member of Parliament. Only burgess votes were counted; this elevated small-town politics to the national level at each infrequent election.

Walpole relied on the Argyll faction after the union and the house of Argyll and its supporters reached their zenith of power in the mid century. A second Whig group, 'the Squadrone', also supported the government, but distrusted Argyll's men. The third political element was the disaffected episcopalian Jacobites who gained little power but posed a mild threat. As his manager for Scotland Walpole appointed the Earl of Islay (who later succeeded as Third Duke of Argyll). Only a man with deep knowledge of Scottish affairs could hope to command. Control was ensured by the customary eighteenth-century system of patronage, by which every appointment, at every level of society, was made through the recommendation of some greater man. Islay remained at the apex of this pyramid until 1761, presiding over increasing prosperity and stability. The Jacobite risings came and went and the country settled to peace, and prosperity for the Whig landowners, supporters of the House of Hanover and of moderate presbyterianism.

The eighteenth and early nineteenth centuries were, in Scotland as elsewhere in Britain, a period of intense change and of industrial development. The greatest change, largely hidden at the time, was the steady and spectacular upsurge in the population of Scotland, part of the general upsurge of European populations. This began about the middle of the eighteenth century and accelerated in subsequent decades. In 1755 the population of Scotland was estimated to have

112

been about 1.2 million, half of them living north of the Forth. By 1841 it had more than doubled to 2.6 million and by 1871 it was 3.3 million. By far the greatest concentrations of population by then were found in the formerly empty uplands of Lanarkshire, in the Clyde basin and in the central belt between Forth and Clyde. The causes of this increase in population are multiple and still not understood in complete detail.

One result of the increase in population was that people became much more mobile. Great movements took place, though few were mass movements. Family units moved to better employment or to the apparent promise of betterment; some were thrust out by pressure from landlords or stark economics, others willingly moved towards the new towns and mills which offered prospects of wages for the whole family. The static society of the past, anchored to the land or to the small burghs, began to change and the pace of change increased. In the end this mobility posed a greater threat to the Whig landowner's ascendancy than did any rebellious Jacobite.

The land and the landlords

On the majority of estates in the first half of the eighteenth century agricultural changes came gradually, and only a handful of enthusiasts spent time and money on experimental farming. The main change taking place was the replacement of commonly held ferm-touns by single-tenant farms. One farmer paying a high rent was becoming more desirable than a handful of tenants farming in common. These changes took place smoothly in Lothian and on Lowland farms. Agricultural surpluses were increasing and more mixed farming was attempted all over Scotland. Grass parks for stock were enclosed: roots and beans were beginning to be cultivated. In spite of these germs of progress traditional practices still predominated.

In the Highlands the existing system made use of a middleman, the tacksman, who held a large tract of land from the principal owner who was usually a relative and head of the family. The tacksman sublet at high rates to cottars who farmed the land. The second Duke of Argyll saw that this system was unprofitable to the landowner, and attempted to eliminate the tacksman and form big farms. This caused great alarm in clan Campbell, one of the most cohesive and interrelated of Highland groups. Confidence in leadership was shaken and drastic agricultural changes were delayed for a generation.

Industries were still based on natural products; the dominant manufactures of Scotland were textiles. Nearly every household spun its own wool and linen yarn; hand-weavers were to be found in most towns, and especially concentrated in Fife, east Perthshire and in Ayrshire. In 1727 a Board of Trustees for Fisheries and Manufactures in Scotland was set up, and chiefly encouraged the linen industry. Flax seed and dressed flax were imported from Europe to supplement the domestic growth. Flax was an unpopular new crop, as its cultivation and processing were laborious. The linen industry, under encouragement, grew and prospered, and contributed indirectly to the increase in rents that every landowner wished to see. Coal and other minerals were developed whenever possible and mines with long adits were being driven deeper, by landowners whose property had easily-worked deposits. Demand for coal grew, not only in the towns and for export but also for infant industries, particularly for lime kilns and the saltpans that supplied the requirements of the fishing industry. After union the pull of colonial needs began to be felt; salt herring and coarse linen sold well in the slave-owning southern colonies of America and the West Indies.

In the eighteenth century distilling of whisky began to move from being a cottage process to an industrial one, as brewing had already done in the cities. Gradually whisky became a socially acceptable drink as it was better made, and became not merely a fiery and coarse domestic product for the consolation of the 'lower orders' or to provide 'the fastest road out of Glasgow'. English insistence on the malt tax, on the licensing of stills and on a minimum maturation period was much resented but did contribute to an improved product, as did Highland shooting parties and officers' messes who acquired the taste. Another encouragement was the early emergence of the brand-name. Ownership of the distillery at Ferintosh, near Dingwall, was one of the gains of the Whig family of Forbes of Culloden after the rising of 1715, and its malt became justly famous.

Most of the licensed distilleries were situated north of the Highland Line (a line which was first legally drawn in 1785, for Excise purposes). So were the illicit stills. In 1782 over eight hundred illicit stills were seized in the Lowlands, and 1121 in the Highlands. The Exciseman took a high place in any list of unpopular local characters. Highlanders were inclined to consider that selling the product of their own domestic stills was a right and the only way to make a little cash for the rents, a matter which landowning magistrates found difficult to judge; they often compromised by setting very low fines for those convicted of running a still.

Whisky distilling was one of the few industries to thrive in remote Highland and Island districts, providing wages for the men of small communities, especially after the legislation of 1822 and 1823 made legitimate distilling profitable. The local consumption of cheap whisky by man, woman and child was very high, as Jane Grant noted in Speyside in 1814. It cost about one halfpenny for a half-gill. Barley for malting could not be grown in sufficiency in Scotland, and was imported. For three dreadful years during the height of the Napoleonic wars distilling of barley was banned to conserve imports of grain, but fortunately large stocks of molasses in Greenock enabled rum production to proceed unchecked. After the war with France the exports of whisky in cask (accompanied by empty bottles and clean corks in the same shipment) figure in the export cargoes of ships bound from the Clyde to all ports where migrant Scots would guarantee good sales. Production steadily increased.

Partly as a result of the Malt Tax and the profit to be made from illicit whisky, and partly as a result of penal taxation on luxuries such as tea and necessities such as salt, smuggling could rank as a Scottish industry.

Deference

Perhaps the notable social characteristic of the countryside, as of the whole of Britain in the eighteenth century, was the habit of deference. The 'natural order' was accepted without question, a hierarchy of the propertied who kept law and order in a country without any police force. The kirk reinforced deferential behaviour, inculcating obedience and a moral discipline on the people. The heritors, the men of property in each parish, bore responsibility for the choice of minister (under powers of patronage restored by the Patronage Act of 1712 and much resented by the radical Presbyterians). Heritors also bore the cost of parish schools. They thus controlled appointment of both minister and dominie (schoolmaster) and their choices fell on the men who upheld the system and showed sufficient deference. By the mid century these accommodating ministers formed an identifiable Moderate party. Small splinter groups detached themselves from the kirk in protest, in the Original Secession of 1733.

The parish schools, if they encouraged the habits of deference and obedience, also gave good basic education to all classes and both sexes in the countryside. Burgh schools, under local control, gave education to boys, and from both backgrounds able boys could progress to one of the Scottish universities. At the beginning of the century the tradition of proceeding to Europe to complete education was still widespread. A leaven of intellectual inquiry was beginning to ferment in Scottish universities, working in the solid scholarship already established.

The Jacobites' last risings

Despite the dullness of politics and the deferential studiousness of much of the country, high feelings were generated by the questions of the legitimacy of government and of the presbyterian establishment, posed by the Jacobite, episcopalian and Roman Catholic elements. These elements were mostly found concentrated in the Highlands and Aberdeenshire. Here, deference took the more primitive form of following the head of the family; policing, however, was emphatically undertaken by government. The polarization of the country into mutually hostile Highlands and Lowlands was completed by General Wade who had advanced into the north after the rising of 1715. General Wade's name is now associated with the roads and bridges which his troops drove through to make the north accessible to marching men of the government forces. He was also, though, associated with the Disarming Act of 1716, forbidding the carrying of weapons. Wade commanded an army of occupation, garrisoning Fort William, building Fort Augustus and installing new army posts at Bernera on the north-west coast, Ruthven in upper Speyside and Inversnaid on the marches of the Lowlands. Wade billeted himself in Brahan Castle whose owner Seaforth was in exile overseas after his particularly inept part in the further Jacobite rising in 1719. (Seaforth received a pardon and managed to return to his property after betraying all the details of another attempted rising, in 1725, to the English government (who knew all about it anyway).

One of Wade's English officers, Captain Burt, wrote a bestseller years after his return from the north, about the extreme wildness of the country and the hideous, dirty and impoverished natives it was his ill luck to police. Burt is still much quoted though it is difficult to know how reliable he was. What he was observing was the breakdown of the old pastoral and patriarchal pattern under severe economic distress. The desire of the chiefs to have big followings of fighting men was being replaced by an urge to build big mansion houses and to repair to the court or the fashionable life of London, Bath or the grand tour. Few rent-rolls in Scotland and none in the north were equal to supporting such a lifestyle and rents started to spiral upwards. Nearly all the work of the pastoral communities of the Highlands was done by the womenfolk, with the men annually driving cattle to the great and growing cattle trysts of Doune, Dunblane, Crieff and Falkirk. The only other activity these men of the Celtic twilight would happily engage in was fighting, and the new smooth race of chiefs was disinclined for such ancestral pastimes. Blood feuding was over, but cattle droving flourished and occasional raiding was still known. A sentimental attachment to the exiled House of Stewart went with the strongly held episcopalian sympathies of the majority in the north and a few households kept up a clandestine correspondence with James Edward and his impoverished followers in Urbino or Rome.

Episcopalian ministers still went the rounds, banned by the government as Non-Jurors who would not swear allegiance to King George, but welcomed by their flocks. Whereas in the Lowlands in Queen Anne's day any minister of faintly episcopalian tendency was 'rabbled' and turned out of his kirk by the ferociously presbyterian populace, in the north and the north-west some brisk and equally intolerant episcopalian mobs successfully 'rabbled' the few Presbyterians who attempted to 'intrude'. Repetition of a liturgy, even of the Lord's Prayer, distinguished the Episcopalians from the Presbyterians. It was this surviving division of religious sympathy far more than loyalty to the House of Stewart, which nourished the numerous Jacobite intrigues, landings and risings in the years between 1715 and 1745. The other thing which kept the Stewart cause alive was its occasional value as an irritant, no more than that, in international politics. The continuing prosperity of Argyll, coupled with Campbell support of the kirk, made for more polarizing hostilities in the north. By 1745, however, there was moderate prosperity and a general acceptance of the House of Hanover; only extremists and a few self-seekers saw any possible gain by open support of the Stewart cause unless strongly supported by French aid and English participation.

Into this comparatively tranquil scene news of the landing of Prince Charles Edward Stewart in Moidart in August 1745 sounded like thunder out of a clear sky. Ever since George II had defeated the armies of France at the Battle of Dettingen in 1743 the likelihood of France again encouraging a Jacobite diversion

was strongly and widely acknowledged. But even the stoutest Jacobites were realistically against attempting a rising unless French help were forthcoming. Old James Edward in Rome wrote to Paris pleading with his young son Prince Charles to believe neither the promises of France, after the death of Cardinal Fleury, nor the reports of Jacobite agents and adventurers in Paris, who told the prince tales of fantastic support awaiting him. Adversity had made the Old Chevalier cautious, but the Young Chevalier was not. French political and military aid did fail, and English agents gave the government a fairly accurate forecast of events. In spite of that the prince rashly embarked without French aid in two ships belonging to a Nantes privateer and chased by the Royal Navy which turned back one vessel. The prince and seven companions won through to Scotland, without gold or arms. From Moidart he dispatched peremptory letters demanding the adherence of the leading men of the north, causing great heartsearchings and divisions within families and clans. Duncan Forbes of Culloden, Lord Advocate and leading Whig, desperately tried to hold the loyalty of leading men to the government.

The hard days of the Forty-five

The rising of 1745 did not directly affect the whole of Scotland, and did not, at the time, provide material for song and legend. That came later. It was a hard and painful time, particularly for families of old Jacobite allegiance. The prince's summons was answered by some, in honour bound; others, equally honourably, stood by the established government and the House of Hanover. The Highlanders were more committed to rebellion against the existing order than the Lowlanders were, as a consequence of Wade's military occupation, and the hostility of the administration. The prince's arrival was greeted with exasperation in some quarters, particularly in the south-west of Scotland, the old covenanting stronghold.

By the end of August 1745 a small Highland Jacobite army with Prince Charles Edward at its head marched south, going by Wade's road over the Corrieyairack pass and outwitting General Cope, who commanded the government forces and had hurried to Inverness via Huntly. At Perth the prince gathered more adherents and advanced to Edinburgh, outflanking the garrison of Stirling Castle. South of the Forth far fewer supporters came in, though for six weeks the Highland host occupied Edinburgh (with the exception of the Castle) and the prince received the loyal and curious in the old family palace of Holyrood. When General Cope returned from the north he was beaten by the Jacobite army at a brisk engagement outside the city at Prestonpans. The prince's army then marched for England. Few English Jacobites joined him, Manchester alone providing recruits. Flaws and quarrels over strategy developed. The prince and the Irish advisors he had brought with him took a different line from Lord George Murray, the Jacobite Chief of Staff. The government's countermeasures were becoming a threat to the Jacobite army. A well-trained force, containing regiments which were experienced veterans of Dettingen and recent campaigns on the Continent, was marching north to meet them, commanded by the Duke of Cumberland, son of George II. Some of these regiments were Lowland Scottish.

In London news of the advance of Prince Charles Edward to Derby started a run on the Bank of England and engendered great alarm. This turned to rejoicing when the news followed that the Highland forces had turned back and were retreating north again. That night the Drury Lane Theatre hastily put together new words to an old tune and brought the house down with 'God save the King'.

The Duke of Cumberland and Prince Charles

The prince in retreat

The Jacobite forces retreated north-west through Carlisle and Glasgow (where their reception was frosty) and across to Falkirk where they met and defeated the advance party of the government forces but failed to take Stirling Castle. Cumberland reached Edinburgh and marched north scarcely a week behind the retreating Highlanders who were making for Inverness. A short foray of forced marching along the Moray coast reflected the indecision in Jacobite leadership. Rumours of the arrival of French help were widespread but the seas were efficiently patrolled by the Royal Navy and no help came. On 16 April 1746 the exhausted and hungry Jacobite forces were drawn up on a moor near Inverness, behind Duncan Forbes's house of Culloden as it happened, for a full-scale engagement. They met the withering fire of the Hanoverian army before they could make their bare-steel charge. It was all over in half an hour.

Before the prince could be spirited away to France, after Culloden, he spent four months in hiding in the north-west of the Highlands and in the Hebrides. There was a price of £30,000 on his head and the severest penalties for sheltering him, but he was not betrayed.

The Jacobite rising of 1745 had only two assets, one of which still shines while the other tarnished rapidly. The first was the conduct of the Highland Jacobites who joined out of a sense of duty and suffered, after defeat, with dignity and pride. The other asset, the enormous personal charm of Prince Charles Edward, sadly turned to pinchbeck before the eyes of his supporters once he had returned to the Continent. It became apparent that he had no lasting qualities of leadership; adversity turned him petulant and suspicious. He died long after, in Rome in 1788; his younger brother Henry, Cardinal-Duke of York had, by going into the church, given up any claim to the throne of Britain. The Stewart cause never again gave any alarm to subsequent governments of Great Britain. George IV paid for a handsome marble monument to be placed in St Peter's, Rome, to the memory of the last of the Stewart line.

The sentimental songmaking is a part of the later myth of Bonny Prince Charlie—'Charlie is my darling, the Young Chevalier'; this came late in the century. At the time, few wrote memorable verse. A few lines of a soldier of the King of France who returned to take part in the whole campaign, and wrote in Gaelic, give a hint of the bitterness of the aftermath:

> My great grief, the white bodies
> that lie on the hills over there
> without coffin or shroud,
> or burial even in holes!
> Those that still live have scattered,
> and are now herded close on the ships.
> The Whigs got their own way,
> and 'Rebels' is what we are called.
>
> John Roy Stewart

120

X

The late Eighteenth Century

Edinburgh and the Enlightenment

THE UNION OF Parliaments left Scotland in an uneasy and benumbed state, partly emasculated. At the same time the religious debates quietened into a broad acceptance of the Presbyterian Church of Scotland By Law Established, as guardian of the nation's morals and, in its annual Assembly, a debating forum for the social problems of the day. Public life, however, became increasingly secular. By slow degrees the economic prospects improved. In the main agricultural sector a handful of gentry pursued expensive schemes of experimental improvement which gradually began to pay off and be copied. The energies of those who during the previous century had concentrated on politics, religion and open warfare now turned to the wider groupings of public life: the law, the universities, the commerce of the west and the development of the burghs. Model villages were built, and by the end of the century a great improvement in the standards of rural building and of enclosed farms was noticeable. The two most important features of Scottish life in the eighteenth century were the great changes made in farming, resulting in a food surplus and a market which eventually covered the whole country and defeated most famines, and in the steady silent growth in population.

There was, however, at the beginning of the century a lack of nerve, of confidence in being Scots. This is a little difficult to define, but is most clearly demonstrated in the great decline in native Scots literature. Written English was the only acceptable form, and Scots found themselves struggling to express themselves in a written form that differed from the spoken word of everyday speech. The English had an unfortunate tendency to mock the Scots, and the Scotch joke or gibe about meanness goes back at least to the arrival of James VI's impoverished nobles in England. John Donne, Dean of St Paul's, wrote a bitter pen picture of these first Scots in London:

> . . . one onley cloak for the rain, which yet he made him serve for all weathers: A Barren half-acre of Face, amidst whereof an eminent Nose advanced itself . . . overlooking his Beard and all the wilde Country thereabouts . . . certain dumb creeping followers, yet they made way for their Master, the Laird . . .

121

This patronizing note was sounded again and again until the achievements of the great literati of the eighteenth century made general gibes against the Scots look foolish.

The nobility solved the problem of language and manners by increasing their rents at home and affording to educate their sons in England; lesser folk simply had to take care how they wrote. There was a peak of criticism of the Scots after the last Jacobite rising had proved how 'unpatriotic' some of them were. In 1760 young King George III came to the throne, with his extremely unpopular tutor raised to the rank of his first Prime Minister, confidant of the king and of his mother. This was Lord Bute, an anglicized Scot, but a Scot. Attacks on him took the form of a general derision of the Scots, and this was brought to a high pitch of vilification by John Wilkes. He published a crudely satirical paper called *The North Briton*, which established important principles of the freedom of the press, but did nothing for the good name of the Scots. This may have dried up the writing of sensitive souls. Some writers went south and became so anglicized that it is difficult to deduce the Scottish origins of the novelist Tobias Smollett and poet James Thomson from their work. A worthy of Aberdeen University, Professor Beattie, produced a useful handbook for his students entitled *Scotticisms, arranged in Alphabetical Order, designed to correct Improprieties of Speech and Writing*, which enjoyed good sales so late as the last quarter of the eighteenth century.

From all these seedbeds, including contempt, came the intellectual flowering which is called the Scottish Enlightenment, and neatly labelled 1750-80, though its effects were noticeable for long after. Like all labels this is a facile one, though some name must be given to the outpouring of philosophy and practical science, architecture and medicine which lit up the eighteenth century's intellectual life. The Enlightenment did not come suddenly, it grew slowly from the time of the Restoration of Charles II, and it was a European phenomenon in which Scotland played the leading British part.

Education

Naturally education was an important factor. Various Acts to establish parochial schools had been passed through the old Scots Parliament since 1616, obedient to Knox's teaching. The 1696 Act for Settling of Schools spurred on those heritors who had not yet provided schools to do so, and gave some status and security to the lowly schoolmasters. The burghs had established secondary grammar schools, and later many became academies, teaching practical subjects for middle-class boys. Only in the Highlands were the parishes so vast that one school in each could do little good. After the early Jacobite risings had alarmed the rest of the country a charitable movement was set on foot to educate Highland children in the necessary knowledge of Presbyterian beliefs, the catechism, arithmetic and the English language. This would inculcate loyalty to church and state and enable emigrants to find work more easily. Scottish Society for Promoting

Christian Knowledge (SSPCK) schools or 'English' schools, subscribed to by good Lowlanders, did missionary work in education along these lines—though attendance was thin during the summer herding season. No education was totally free, though all was subsidized and available. The overall result was widespread literacy. The little lending library of Innerpeffery, in Perthshire, shows farm workers reading theology and philosophy. This library was left for the use of the parish by a Restoration law lord, Lord Madderty, and rehoused in 1764; the readers' registers begin then.

The Scottish universities were naturally at the apex of the system. In the eighteenth century Edinburgh emerged as the pacemaker. Edinburgh University was a post-Reformation foundation supported by the town council. It attracted professors from other universities by its status and by the good terms offered. Payment was by class fees payable by each student, reinforcing the standing of the good or popular lecturers who attracted big classes. The regenting system was abolished early in the eighteenth century, by which one academic had been responsible for the teaching of all subjects; lectures too henceforward were in English, not Latin. Though the teaching of the classics had a great place, these were not overemphasized in the current English manner. Mathematics was an honoured subject.

How much the universities were directly responsible for the Enlightenment is impossible to gauge. While it is possible to point to the great increase in university subjects taught, and to the number of students attending, it is not so easy to determine whether this was a cause or a result of the general enlightenment of the mid-century. A great number of clubs and societies in which men of like interests met, in Edinburgh and Glasgow, had perhaps as formative an effect on the intellectual life of Scotland as the universities did. Scottish society was close knit and the universities were one important component.

The literati: the original thinkers

In 1729 Francis Hutcheson came from Ulster to the chair of Moral Philosophy in Glasgow, and taught that the law of God could be seen in the workings of Nature, and that virtue could be defined as agreeing with this harmony. He also first formulated 'that action is best which procures the greatest happiness for the greatest numbers, and that worst which in like manner occasions misery'. It was scarcely traditional Presbyterian teaching, but it deeply influenced the philosophers of the next generation, and the students for the ministry who became the mid-century Moderates. Hutcheson ushered in the secular approach of the Age of Reason.

The Enlightenment itself was the work of a handful of original thinkers or literati, of whom David Hume (1711-72) was by far the most outstanding, supported by and interacting with his friends Adam Smith, Professor Cullen and Doctor Black, the Reverend Principal Robertson, and others only slightly less distinguished. Hume, the philosopher, was and still is a figure of international stature, but his roots were in Scotland and in a sense he restated the persistent Calvinist problem of the relation between man, God, and the state. He took the discussion much further, concentrating on the relationship between man and God, and on the very nature of God. This by a paradox led him to reflect deeply on the nature of man. Hume published his *Treatise of Human Nature* in London in 1738. He classified himself as a 'mitigated sceptic' though his contemporaries thought of him as a dangerously radical sceptic: he argued that if God was incomparable man should in all humility bend his intellect, his reason, to the guidance of his own conduct. To Hume the unacceptable alternative to self-knowledge was the unreasoning blind acceptance of a God only too obviously made in man's image. Hume lived in Europe, in some renown, but came home to Edinburgh in his old age, shunned by the kirk and regarded with apprehension by the university; he divided his time between philosophy and cooking little meals in the French style for his close friends. His arguments about social man were based on scientific methods of proof ultimately derived from Newton's *Principia*. Newtonian theory, early in the century, revolutionized thought and teaching in Scotland before gaining general acceptance in England.

Another group who contributed to the Enlightenment were the chemists who, with the medical doctors, made striking contributions to the extension of knowledge. William Cullen trained as a doctor of medicine but turned his attention to chemistry and to the current state of knowledge of the physical properties of matter. He was a successful teacher at Glasgow University and moved to Edinburgh in 1756, where again his lectures became immensely popular. His interest extended into practical topics such as soil chemistry analysis (never before attempted), the action of fertilizers and the assessment of natural mineral deposits. All these were of interest to improving landlords. He and his pupil and successor Doctor Black worked on such topics, but his greatest fame lies in his experiments to determine the nature of heat. When Black took over Cullen's chair in Glasgow he concentrated his research on this and eventually formulated his theory of latent heat. It was less a theory than a discovery of properties and a quantification of previously uncharted phenomena; it was new and startling.

Dr Joseph Black

In Black's time his friend and collaborator James Watt was working from 1758 onward on the practical application of the Cornish Newcomen steam engine as a pump for coal mines. Using Black's method and approach and some of Cullen's experiments Watt quite separately arrived at devising the separate steam condenser. This invention and Watt's subsequent modifications ensured that first the stationary steam engine and later the mobile locomotive were developed to revolutionize the energy input of the world. Watt left Scotland to go into partnership with Matthew Boulton of Birmingham to manufacture steam engines. The technology then available in Birmingham was more advanced than any Scottish manufacturer could match, and thus the crucial development of the steam engine is a child of both Scottish and English parentage.

Of the other literati Adam Smith is also a world figure. He, like Hume, was preoccupied with social man, with the rules and moral sanctions that differentiated man from beast, and made societies. Whereas Hume looked at social questions as a philosopher Smith drew on more specifically historic illustrations, and attempted analysis. *The Wealth of Nations* is more than the first work of economic analysis, it is also a product of Scottish social philosophy, and a general interest in the past. Smith's and Hume's interest in history was characteristic of the Enlightenment. Principal Robertson of Edinburgh University had become, after Gibbon, the most distinguished historian of the day, and widely read. The publishers of the day offered large advances for works which might be thought controversial, secure in the public demand for intellectual debate. This interest in historical processes led Hume into philosophy, Smith into economics and Adam Ferguson and John Millar towards sociology: uncharted territories.

Perhaps the most typical if not the most notable figure of the Enlightenment was Henry Home-Drummond, Lord Kames, whose long life almost spans the eighteenth century. He was the son of a Border bonnet-laird and went into the law, where he showed little early ability. He worked hard, joined the Whig clubs and, to bring his name before the public, wrote a number of books on philosophy and social law. These were neither as original nor as entertaining as his friend David Hume's work but the public found them less alarming and easier to assimilate. He enjoyed considerable success with *Principles of Equity* in 1760 and *Elements of Criticism* two years later. The patronage of the Duke of Argyll made him a Lord of Session, put him on the Board of Trustees for Fisheries and Manufactures and made him a Commissioner for the Forfeited Annexed Estates, all of which he served diligently. A happy marriage late in life to a Drummond heiress brought him to a big estate on the flat waterlogged Carse of Stirling. He became enthusiastic for improvement, and put into effect all the theory of the age, with good results. He drained the mossy land by a complicated canal system flushed by an Egyptian waterwheel; he installed displaced Highlanders as tenants, planted timber for future utility, made his own roof tiles and paid for a school. He asked Professor Black to join his house parties and to advise on soil and perform tests to determine its quality; Benjamin Franklin also came to stay, describing his visit as 'six weeks of the *densest* happiness'. Kames wrote on agricultural improvement, and in his old age gives the impression of a truly rounded man of the Augustan age. When he laid out his orchard at Blair Drummond he asked his neighbour Ramsay of Ochtertyre for an inscription for an obelisk that he was erecting at the end of the vista. Ramsay supplied an epigram inspired by David Hume:

> Graft Benevolence on Self-love
> The Fruit will be Delicious

It is the authentic voice of the Scottish Enlightenment, the Age of Reason, when with a little self-discipline man might become perfectible and natural justice and morality could order an orchard. It can also be read as foreshadowing the hard commercial morality, combined with private charity, of the early industrialists.

In another field, not far removed, James Hutton was laying the foundations of modern geology. James Hutton was a member of many clubs in Edinburgh, but not of the university; he sent his 'Theory of the Earth' to the Royal Society in 1785. Without labouring the point Hutton quietly threw overboard the accepted Biblical story of the creation of the earth in seven days and postulated that the earth's surface had developed very slowly through the action of erosion and water, volcanic eruption and internal heat. Hutton had considered the work of Cullen and Black and applied it theoretically on a global scale. He put more emphasis on the constant ageing changes at work on the earth's crust than on creation; however, later a titanic battle arose between his school of Huttonians and Professor Jameson, a follower of Werner, who tried to fit the evidence of the rocks into a scriptural timetable. When asked to account for a fossil fish found deep in a coal seam one of the Wernerian school tried to argue that God had put it there as a test of belief. The debate raged long, and was the cause of agonizing internal debates in university and theological circles. The legacy of these great figures was not only enlarged horizons, but the discipline of inquiry and of scientific research. These engendered passionate and partisan argument of which the Huttonian debate is a good example. Edinburgh became noted for its teaching, publishing, and for its lively intellectual life; many students from the rest of Europe came there, and booksellers flourished.

Edinburgh New Town

The old town of Edinburgh lay on the ridge running straight from the Castle down the spine of the Royal Mile to Holyroodhouse. Little wynds led off the main road, on each side, like the backbone of a fish. Queen Mary's old walls roughly defined the city limits, and life was led in crowded conditions, in 'high-rise' tenements. Social mixing was complete. There were no drains and only a scanty water supply. By the middle of the century these conditions began to affront the well-born and there was little space for the meetings of the many societies and clubs, beyond the taverns which were such a lively feature of the old town. Robert Fergusson, one of the first poets after a long stifled silence, was not afraid to write in Scots of the life he observed, and briefly lived to the full. He wrote of Edinburgh's Hallow Fair in 1772:

At Hallowmas, whan nights grow lang,	At Hallowe'en when the nights grow long
And stannies shine fu' clear,	And stars shine out clearly
Whan fock, the nippin cald to bang,	When folk, the nipping cold to thwart
Their winter hap-warms wear,	Wear their warm winter wraps,
Near Edinborough a fair there hads,	A fair is held, near Edinburgh—
I wat there's nane whase name is,	I bet there is not one better known—
For strapping dames and sturdy lads	For strapping girls and sturdy lads
And cap and stoup, mair famous	And food and drink—there's none more famous
Than it that day.[1]	Than that fair-day.

Old Edinburgh was teeming with life, but never genteel.

The Town Council proposed to build a speculative New Town, on the further side of the Nor' Loch, for the comfort and convenience of citizens and winter visitors, especially of the professional and middle classes. They held a competition and in 1767 gave the prize to James Craig for his overall design. Building started, and continued for more than a generation. The moving spirit was Provost Drummond, a Whig from a Perthshire Jacobite background who managed to establish himself in the tightly knit Town Council and to be elected six times as Provost. He was thus ex-officio chancellor of 'The Town's College' as the university was often called. He left his mark on the development of the university as well as the town, particularly on the expansion of the medical school and the building of the Royal Infirmary. Drummond's great influence on the Edinburgh of the Enlightenment was thus structural and external. Edinburgh New Town was designed to attract more gentry into the city, and her good educational establishments and health facilities would do the same. The town councils of both Edinburgh and Glasgow were alike in being self-perpetuating closed circles, much reviled by the rest of the populace, and appearing to be only interested in promoting the narrow interests of the merchants. But they presided over important social changes. The New Town gave a formal setting of Georgian elegance to the second generation of enlightened Scotsmen. The original literati were to be found in the taverns of the Canongate, as their fathers had been, taking a dram and eating mutton pies and talking gloriously.

The arts and the performers

Music in Scotland has so strongly been associated with the vigorous folk tradition of fiddle and pipe playing and the singing of unaccompanied ballads, that the place of classical music has been a little overlooked.

The larger cities of Scotland, however, all seem to have supported musical societies in the eighteenth century, in spite of the previous long years when formal music had lean patronage, with no court and with the active hostility of the kirk. Aberdeen was one such musical town. Attempts to combine music schools with church choirs in the bigger burghs failed, as the kirk disapproved of any singing in which the congregation did not join, and also disapproved of the use of organs. A 'Kist o' Whussles' (organ) was an episcopalian abomination. However, formal music-making never died out of social life.

The Edinburgh Music Society started in the 1690s, but did not flourish until after union, and then only in the winter when the gentry came to the capital, providing an informed audience. Many had learnt music while travelling or staying abroad. They bought sheet music, first published in Edinburgh in 1725, to take back to their country houses, just as they bought Allan Ramsay's *Tea-Table Miscellany*, to remind themselves of Scottish songs and old ballads. Ramsay had tidied these up and brought them back into fashion, treated a little sentimentally. The genius of The Edinburgh Music Society was a splendidly eccentric peer, the Earl of Kellie, who himself composed, conducted, and played several instruments. The library of the society contained a useful number of old orchestral pieces, and the new works of Handel. The society held guest concerts for continental performers, an expensive exercise that was well patronized. Edinburgh was the only centre large enough to support this kind of international musical life, though for some reason at the end of the century interest waned, and the society died in 1798.

Dancing, in assembly rooms all round the country, in private houses and at humble celebrations, was a country-wide pastime. It spanned the range from the formal and genteel to rowdy reeling: neat footwork was always admired. The music was provided by the fiddle for reels and strathspeys, particularly during the long period of mid-century when the playing of the pipes was forbidden to all but the army. For minuets and other foreign dances in polite circles the fiddlers were joined by oboe, bassoon, clarinet and bass viol. Miss Grant of Rothiemurchus in her *Memoirs of a Highland Lady* described country dancing in Speyside, balls in Inverness, and in Edinburgh, where the dancing and concert-going for young ladies just 'out' nearly brought her to a breakdown.

The theatre in the capital also suffered from kirk censure, and the rise of play-going mirrors the decline of the full rigours of kirk morality. No theatre was actually licensed, though the Canongate Concerthall did put on plays, until the Act authorizing the building of the New Town included a theatre patent, in 1767. Neither plays nor opera of high quality seem to have been performed. John

Home's home-grown drama *Douglas* was received rapturously, but that was more a mark of the inexperience of the audience than of the play's quality. By 1784, in the heyday of Moderate ministers, the sessions of the General Assembly itself had to be retimed to enable all those who wished to see the great Mrs Siddons in her first appearance in Scotland. Plays also went on tour, but suffered even more from rural disapproval than in cities.

The painters who worked in Scotland in the eighteenth century were a vigorous school. Earlier tradition supported by Jamesone and Michael Wright had produced generations of family portraits. This tradition was carried on by Allan Ramsay the younger, by David Allan and finally by Raeburn. Gavin Hamilton lived in Rome and was prepared to paint rich patrons leaning negligently on the ruins of antiquity, or to arrange their purchase of fashionable Italian pictures and objets d'art. Another vein was mined by David Wilkie, the first of a long series of genre painters who carried on studies of 'the peasantry' through to Victorian sentimentality—'kailyarders' in paint. The earlier paintings of this school, however, give us valuable insights into the cottage interiors, the fairs, fisher folk and weavers, and the back gardens of Scotland.

Scotland has produced a remarkably fine crop of architects. The first to make a name and fortune for himself was Sir William Bruce, in Restoration days. Unfortunately the relative poverty of the country meant that the best work of many of the later architects was done outside Scotland. When the burgesses of Stirling decided to rebuild the old Town House in 1703 they sent their master mason to Bruce to ask him just to draw a quick elevation, as they could not afford his full plans and supervision. Colen Campbell built Stourhead for an English banker and worked in Germany; Gibbs, an Aberdonian, built a church there and made no charge for doing so, but is better known for St Martin in the Fields and for work for both Oxford and Cambridge. Only a few of the buildings of the most famous Scots architect of all, Robert Adam, were for Scottish patrons. However, these included Mellerstain, Culzean, Register House, plans for Edinburgh University, and the north side of Charlotte Square, Edinburgh, as well as a style stamped indelibly on a whole generation of British architects, furniture makers and fabric designers. Robert Adam's father, William, was one of an earlier and more domestic line of builders, who found a patron in the state. The elder Adam, James Smith and Robert Mylne were all master masons in the state service, though light duties allowed them private practices.

A picture of all the varied life of Edinburgh at the end of the century is conveyed by Lord Cockburn, who begins his *Memorials* as soon after his birth in 1779 as he could remember and takes his gossipy and sensitive observation of the Edinburgh scene up to 1830.

He describes his early schooling and holidays, against a background of the Old Town, and his enrolment at The College (the university).

A debating society was one of the natural results of the classes in Logic and Moral Philosophy. These institutions, when ill-managed, are hotbeds of

130

conceit and petulance, but when managed tolerably well are powerfully productive of thought, of talent, and even of modesty.

Edinburgh during the Enlightenment and its afterglow was indeed powerfully productive of thought and talent.

The growth of Glasgow and the merchants of the west of Scotland

By the middle of the eighteenth century the balance of Scotland was altering, and a new polarity was developing. The contrasts between Highlands and Lowlands remained, but became of far less consequence than the contrasts between Edinburgh and Glasgow, and their respective hinterlands, Lothian, and Lanarkshire and Clyde. Both cities showed growth: Edinburgh became one of the intellectual centres of Europe and Glasgow a leading centre of industry and commerce. Like all generalizations, this must be qualified: there were Glasgow intellectuals and Edinburgh-based industries, but the general patterns of the two cities were widely different. Each in the eighteenth century was in its own way dynamic.

Not all the industrial development of Glasgow was uniquely Scottish, as the industrial revolution spread over the British Isles. The spread of technological innovations is part of the general history of Britain and was a main instrument in welding its various regions, including England and Scotland themselves, into a whole. Improved transport and the technologies of steam power and textile mills did not stop at regional boundaries. Better communications and marketing mechanisms were great unifying factors.

Glasgow, in 1727, according to Daniel Defoe, the English investigative journalist (or spy), was a small and particularly elegant town, built round the university and cathedral on a stream which ran down to the Clyde—a river then in parts only six inches deep, wide and full of salmon. The lively intellectual life was sharpened by presbyterian theology and expressed in good practical Whiggish terms of trade and commerce. Few in Glasgow supported the Jacobites. The Argyll interest was strong. Before the Act of Union, and for years afterwards, Glasgow merchants sent ships and goods from the English port of Whitehaven in Cumbria to America, to take advantage of English trade regulations. Glasgow merchant houses then developed the deepwater port of Greenock and Port Glasgow higher up the Clyde.

By the mid-eighteenth century concentration on one commodity had brought Glasgow an international reputation. Glasgow was the hub of the tobacco trade with Virginia and the southern colonies of America. Two things seem to have aided the merchants: by abstaining directly from the slave trade and sailing straight, and northabout, to America it was possible for the heavy ships of the day

Fairbairn's water wheel at Deanston cotton works

to make two annual sailings between Greenock and America. The ships of London, Bristol and Liverpool went through the Bay of Biscay, picking up slaves or trading with West Africa before making the West Indies, and finally the American coast, in a triangular voyage lasting a year, and managed at the master's discretion. The second advantage taken by the Scots was organizational. In order to relieve the masters of the responsibility of trading at each port, Glasgow merchant houses put young men ashore in Virginia and the Carolinas to run stores, to supply planters' wants, and to buy and have ready for shipment their hogsheads of tobacco. A Greenock West Indiaman needed only to put into port for a couple of weeks' turn-round for the return voyage: all the paperwork was completed by brisk young factors trained in the new academies of the west of Scotland. Planters became heavily indebted to the convenient stores they ran. The need to fill ships outward bound from Greenock with the trade goods required by young growing colonies stimulated much industrialization in the west of Scotland. The factors could sell many things: nails, hammers and axes, iron stoves and cooking pots, food, clothing and shoes for slaves, glass, crockery, bottles, horse harness and axle-bushes, as well as small expensive consignments of books, wine, furniture and carriages. To furnish all this in bulk, small manu-factories grew up in Scotland such as a dozen cobblers making shoes, or a slit-mill, water powered, making nails. The previously hated Navigation Acts now protected the Scots as well as the English, and prevented the American colonies from, say, making their own nails, one of their severe grievances.

132

Of all these trades the Scottish linen textile one was the most flourishing, supported too by demand at home, and controlled by the Linen Board which inspected and stamped home-produced linens, paying a bounty on stamped yardage and another for export—an early example of government encouragement of infant industry. Textile production boomed, especially in the west, and as supplies of locally grown flax became short, the Scots saw the advantage of importing cotton as a substitute. In 1784 Arkwright was invited to Scotland to advise on the building of cotton mills.

Indirectly also another government board, the Fisheries Board, gained from the colonial trade and gave method to the hand-to-mouth Scottish fisher folk. The board offered a bounty on each cask of salt herring stamped and passed as wholesome, and then shipped to feed the slave labour of the colonies. The ships and armies of the day also required salt beef, but Scotsmen still made more money by raising and droving the beasts live over the border than by processing them in Scotland. Virtually no pigs were raised in Scotland—that was left to the Irish; ancient Pictish taboos made pigmeat unacceptable to the Scot. Into this expanding and healthy pattern of trade the American War of Independence broke with possibilities of disaster. The tobacco trade was never the same, but the merchants were resilient and turned to other colonial products, to the sugar and spices of the West Indies, and to Canadian timber.

Glasgow had earlier invested in sugar houses, boiling molasses and selling sugar to the sweetest-toothed nation in the world. Coffee, a variety of spices, logs of Honduras mahogany and tropical dyestuffs were also brought in. As most of

133

the tobacco had been re-exported, Glasgow became one of the biggest entrepôts in Britain, passing on colonial goods to Europe. The traditional flavour and pink colouring of German sausages was due to German purchases of red pimento, imported through Glasgow from the West Indies.

The cotton revolution

By 1800 seven huge water-powered cotton mills (derived from Arkwright's patent) in remote country areas were being joined by steam powered city cotton-spinning mills, as fast as Glasgow could raise the capital. The ancillary industries of chemicals for dyeing and finishing were flourishing too. The St Rollox chemical works in Glasgow became the biggest in the world, producing the bleaching powder which had revolutionized and mechanized the tedious process of natural bleaching in fields. One of its partners, experimenting with the by-products of coal tar after gas lighting had been installed in many cotton mills, came up with a waterproofing process, and gave his name to the mackintosh. The early cotton spinners, grafting their yarn production onto the established hand-weaving industry, achieved immediate success. Without the skills of the domestic weavers, practised in linen weaving, the rapid rise in production of cotton piece goods could not have been achieved. Power weaving came a generation later.

The familiarity with European markets contributed to a further Glasgow merchanting success. The French Revolution reverberated round Europe, and

134

one liberty enthusiastically adopted by the women of Europe was liberty of dress. Heavy silks, wigs and stays went out with Marie Antoinette; in came light clinging muslins and Kashmir shawls à la Josephine. Both were the expensive imports of the East India Company monopoly. The cotton masters of the west of Scotland concentrated on spinning finer twists, and set the hand weavers and the Ayrshire girls who did tambour embroidery to copy Indian muslins; the skilled weavers of Paisley began weaving convincing facsimile Kashmiri shawls—Paisley pattern. The results were highly competitive, vying with the imported versions, and were exported to Europe using the same routes as the colonial produce.

By the time Napoleon attempted to close the Continent to British imports, and the British to blockade him and starve him out, the Glasgow cotton merchants were exporting a huge but undisclosed quantity of fine yarns, piece goods, shawls and muslins to Europe—undisclosed, as much of it was smuggled by Glasgow agents based under the protection of the Royal Navy at Heligoland, Gibraltar and Malta. One merchant, Finlay, had 700 agents in Europe in 1806. Nowhere in Napoleon's Europe was there a cotton mill spinning fine yarn, and even Lancashire at that date concentrated on coarser counts. For perhaps fifteen years Glasgow supplied the fashionable world; then competition broke their monopoly. Many fortunes had been made, and once competition became serious and fashion began to swing away from muslins, the Glasgow merchants again diversified, as they had after the tobacco trade had dwindled. Many went into the production of cotton mill machinery, and from there to the general engineering which is a more recent industrial memory.

Clyde development

Until well after the end of the eighteenth century the main Clyde ports remained Greenock and Port Glasgow. The shallow winding Clyde could not sustain the beamy sailing boats of 400 tons displacement which plied the West Indian trade. The deepening of the Clyde was a matter of deep civic concern. There was rivalry between the ports: Port Glasgow was established as far back as 1668 as the official harbour of Glasgow, but Greenock was the head Customs port and until the 1820s had the bulk of the overseas trade; the Greenock Harbour Trustees reinforced their claims by providing improved facilities and dry docks. However, the heavy problems of trans-shipment of goods encouraged Glasgow merchants to improve their port, particularly as increased manufacture demanded the import of raw materials, and the export of coal and pig iron was growing all the time, from the heart of the city.

Three phases of development eventually opened the Clyde as far as Glasgow. From the middle of the century—the first Act of Parliament for deepening the Clyde was passed in 1759—measures were taken to make the channel deeper and narrower by means of quays and shoal removal. Small coasters made their way up river. By the 1780s further work undertaken by John Golbourne of Chester had improved the waterway to the point where ships of 100 tons could (with difficulty) reach Glasgow. Work was again undertaken after John Rennie's report of 1799; and in 1809 the Town Council obtained a third River Improvement Act and set up the Trustees of the Clyde Navigation, to administer the port. By 1836 further dredging and narrowing of the channel increased the depth of water to nearly eight feet at the Broomielaw at neap tides, in the heart of the city. This enabled ships of up to four hundred tons to berth, on spring tides, right upriver. It had cost about £1.5 million over the sixty or so years of concentrated effort. Steam power had come to aid the work, as tugs were necessary to bring ships so far inland, and dredging was made much easier by the use of steam. By mid-Victorian times the depth at Glasgow was about twenty-five feet at low tide.

Another hazard, almost as inhibiting as the shallow river itself, was institutional. There was no Customs House in Glasgow, except a substation at Port Dundas on the Forth-Clyde canal and far distant from the Broomielaw, so no goods could be cleared through Glasgow itself. Long years of pressure on the inert bureaucracy of the day in Edinburgh and London was exerted by the raw-cotton importers, and countered by the wine importers who were quite content with Greenock. Eventually, in 1822, bonded warehouses and Customs officers were installed in Glasgow on the Clyde and the port developed rapidly thereafter. Coal and iron became the chief exports.

The Free Traders of Glasgow

The merchants of Glasgow were a cohesive bunch, forming trade associations from an early date and presenting a united front to the world, though internal quarrels went deep. They were pioneers in the art of putting pressure on central government. Hitherto in the eighteenth century any mercantile pressure on Parliament had been exerted by the City of London only, and the merchants of the outports were unheard. By inventing the Chamber of Commerce in 1783 Glasgow was able to exert corporate pressure; their device has been copied throughout the Western world.

Developing from their challenge to central authority, the Glasgow merchants early became converted to Free Trade, a doctrine in total opposition to the beliefs held in London at the time. Scotland had long memories of the Navigation Acts, and the merchant community of Glasgow joined with Liverpool to orchestrate an attack on the last great monopoly in the country, the East India Company. Concerted canvassing in 1812-13 finally opened the India trade to licensed merchants and in 1816 the first ship was sent off from Greenock, loaded with Scottish goods, to free-trade in Bombay. It was soon followed by regular sailings, and whole shipping lines were devoted to the Indian trade. Twenty years later the Company's China trade monopoly in tea export was also broken through countrywide agitation based in Glasgow. In the next generation Manchester succeeded to leadership, and Free Trade became the order of Victorian Britain. Adam Smith of Kirkcaldy, who had enunciated the principles of free trade and attacked monopolies in the latter half of the eighteenth century in *The Wealth of Nations*, was not, in Glasgow, considered such a daring innovator. 'His theories were the common coffee house talk,' remarked one Glasgow contemporary, adding that Smith had served a little time in one of the merchant houses of Glasgow, so naturally would have picked up sound general principles. The comment is a good example of that distinctively Scots reductive idiom which cuts a man down to size.

Banking

In a connected field the Glasgow merchants were influential: that of banking. Banking in Scotland had begun formally with the chartered banks, the Bank of Scotland, founded in 1695, followed by the Royal Bank in 1727. Both were based in the capital, and were the chosen banks of the ruling landed interests; the Bank of Scotland was said to have Jacobite affiliations, while the Royal was connected with the house of Argyll. Droving and the linen industry began to pose rather different banking requirements from those of the landed gentry, met in part by the British Linen Bank, and by the numerous small private banks often opened by lawyers and merchants in small towns. In Glasgow, however, the first banks were promoted by the major merchants, the Tobacco Lords of the mid-century. These offered loans on merchant business, not exclusively on land, and helped, through bills of exchange, to service the expanding commerce. Unfortunately an attempt to form a bank combining commercial and landed interests, and lending freely to both, came to grief in 1772 with the collapse of the Ayr Bank of Douglas, Heron & Co. All over Scotland a lot of money was lost, and so was confidence, but the banking system benefited by the salutary shock. Joint-stock banks with limited liability were subsequently formed, and their policies, though often thought by conservative Edinburgh bankers to be vigorous to the point of danger, did provide cheap money, a growing service and a flexible one, to industry, trade and agriculture, in the west of Scotland.

Coal, iron and steam power

Reference has already been made to the export of coal from Scotland in the seventeenth century. The earliest coalfields to be developed were round the Firth of Forth, in Fife, the Lothians and at Alloa, and were owned and developed by the landowners. The miners were a closed caste, and suffered severe civic disabilities; they were in fact serfs, sold with the property and forbidden to seek other employment, a tied labour force. The mines were small and relatively shallow, often approached by adits driven horizontally into hillsides. Drainage and ventilation were constant problems, and little improvement in conditions was made in the eighteenth century. By 1799 serfdom was abolished by Act of Parliament, and the use of steam pumping engines was slowly growing. Increased demand for coal was responsible for both improvements, but basically the miners contended with the same problems and used the same primitive methods at the end of the century as they had at the start of the mining industry. Immense quantities were hewn and raised by hand, and often carried by the hands of women and children.

About the time of union in 1707 Scottish coal production was in the region of 500,000 tons a year. By 1800 the output was more like 1.8 million tons, and small pits were being worked in Lanarkshire, though the lack of water transport inhibited much expansion there. The Ayrshire pits had a slight advantage, and Ayr and Irvine became coal-exporting ports. The rapid expansion of the textile industry in the west of Scotland gave impetus to local mining, and to the building of canals to carry the coals. Monklands canal, opened in 1793, brought coal right into Glasgow. Earlier, in 1759, the Carron Company had opened its doors, on a waterway near Falkirk. This was the first large-scale ironworks complex in Scotland, and for 20 years after its founding remained the only one. It was an integrated operation, using local coal and iron ore in its furnaces, and employing the resulting pig iron in its own foundries, forges and slitting mills.

By the 1780s the demand for iron had increased to the point where others competed with Carron, and all these new ironworks were located in the west of Scotland. Their early products were not of high quality, and were used locally. There was a shortage of technical knowledge and a reluctance to innovate. Although it was known that the Lanarkshire measures were deposited in bands of coal and iron ore, the coal was not of high enough quality to smelt the ore easily. In 1828 James Neilson, inventive manager of the Glasgow Gas Works and user of much coal, was asked to consider the problem of the blast applied to furnaces. By heating the blast of air entering the furnaces Neilson revolutionized the coal and iron industry. It dramatically saved fuel, and produced a better grade of iron. In about five years this innovation and other modifications had raised the Scottish industry from an uncompetitive local production to one which produced good pig iron more cheaply than anywhere else in Britain. The acute problem of labour to hew coal and iron ore and to work in the new furnaces and foundries was solved by the massive movements of Irish and Highland labour, a displaced peasantry who flooded into the new towns, creating a distinctive pattern of life in formerly empty uplands.

Transport

The transport of goods and men was one of the outstanding improvements of the early nineteenth century. Canals, a proven success in England, were cut, but the geography of Scotland is as unfavourable as that of France to canals, and these contributed comparatively little to Scottish mobility. The private-enterprise Forth-Clyde canal, and the Union, linking with Edinburgh, were the most successful; the two strategic canals, the Caledonian and the Crinan, built with government money to link arms of the sea, remain monuments to the work of the great engineer Thomas Telford, but their traffic has never been much more than coastal ships, fishing boats and pleasure craft. What made them obsolete as they were built was the increase in size of naval shipping, and the advent of the steam packet.

Coastal trade had always been a lifeline; in increased prosperity it expanded, and played a vital role in linking the small ports of the east with Leith and of the west with the Clyde, and both with England. Coal, timber and foodstuffs were the chief cargoes.

Road transport developed late. Till the end of the eighteenth century, outside Edinburgh and the Lothians no one bothered to keep a coach as it was not possible to use it. In the capital itself sedan chairs portered by a race of hardy Highlanders conveyed the polite world about their affairs; elsewhere men rode or used packhorses. Gradually both the public and the administration acted to improve roads. Local endeavour on the part of heritors, aided by government grants, resulted in a network of new roads being constructed. Many were supervised or designed by the Government Surveyor, Thomas Telford, who is said to have been responsible for over seven hundred miles of road and a thousand bridges, besides harbours and 'Parliamentary' churches. In the Lowlands the English example of toll roads was adopted, and regular coach services were instituted. The Glasgow Chamber of Commerce pressed for a direct road link with England, instead of via Edinburgh, and achieved the Elvanfoot road through the upper Clyde valley and by Beattock to Carlisle (the present M74). News from London could now reach Glasgow or Edinburgh in under thirty-six hours.

A more fundamental change was brought about by steam. Although James

Watt's initial innovations were made in Scotland, and coal pits at Alloa and Tranent had been linked to the sea wharfs by railways since about 1722, Scotland was not in the forefront of railway development and most of the earliest lines for passenger traffic were laid by engineers from Gateshead and the Tyne. Two small local lines, however, the Monkland Line (1826) and the Glasgow and Garnkirk (1831) were opened near Glasgow and competed successfully with the adjacent canal. Edinburgh and Glasgow were soon linked by rail, and from that line the Scottish Central Railway ran to Perth. Other connections followed in the 1840s but it was another generation before Inverness or Thurso were railheads. The contractors for the Scottish Central Railway were also laying the first railway in France, from Le Havre to Paris, and exporting huge quantities of Scottish pig iron from Glasgow. Railways, it has been calculated, consumed 1.5 million tons of iron in the period of greatest expansion between 1846 and 1850. The shift from textiles to heavy industry in the west of Scotland was marked, and shipbuilding made its contribution.

Shipbuilding

Steamship building on the Clyde did not develop out of a great concentration of wooden shipbuilding, but as a new skill based on the craft of boilermakers and platelayers and practical men who could apply new theories to new uses. One of the first vessels was the *Charlotte Dundas*, a paddlesteamer on the Forth-Clyde canal whose speed was so great that the banks crumbled, and she had to be laid up, in 1802. Ten years later Henry Bell built the *Comet* by employing various specialist craftsmen, and it successfully plied on Clyde waters. The *Comet* was followed by a generation of paddledriven steam packets. In the next 20 years foundries made steam boilers and shipyards made wooden ships and installed them.

By the 1830s other areas of Britain had caught up with these comparatively simple skills, but the Clyde took the lead again with rapid advances in the technology of marine engines. The Napier family improved the efficiency of boilers in a series of brilliant innovations. By 1840 nearly a quarter of Britain's steam tonnage was Clyde built and the industry continued to expand as increased efficiency gave steamers a greater range. A second great innovation was the screw, or propeller, first tried in 1840, and a third the introduction of the compound marine engine, experimentally made in America and Germany but commercially pioneered by Clyde engineers from about 1853. It dramatically reduced coal consumption. At the same time the increased size of ships, possible because of the power available, threw such strains on wooden hulls that iron ships soon dominated. *Fire Queen* launched in 1845 was the first of the Clyde-built iron screwdriven steamers; she had 135 tons displacement and developed 80 h.p. Iron replaced wooden hulls, and the Clyde with the ready supplies of coal and iron, and the trained men and engineers made her shipping industry into the leading sector in Scotland.

The Highlands from the Forty-five to the clearances

The months after the battle of Culloden were disfigured by military brutality, and the paying off of old scores by a few less scrupulous citizens. The Disarming Act of 1746 prohibited the carrying of weapons and wearing of Highland dress, except under permit. Known or suspected rebels were hunted out, and in some glens whole townships were burnt, and cattle and horses carried off to supply the occupying troops. Captured rebels were taken to Carlisle to be tried before English juries. Gradually and creakingly the civil government took over from the military, at a speed which reflected the lack of interest in Highland affairs after the general relief at the ending of the Jacobite rising simmered down. The most important piece of legislation passed as a result of the rising was The Abolition of Heritable Jurisdictions Act of 1747. It was thought that the wide civil rights enjoyed by many landowners in Scotland through their courts of Barony and Regality contributed to rebellion, through the powers held over tenants. Perhaps half of Scotland was subject to heritable jurisdictions, and the measure removing this privilege from heritors was deeply resented in the Whig Lowlands as much as in the more volatile north. Even Argyll lost his Heritable Regality.

Apart from the disgruntled heritors who were paid compensation for their loss of 'pit and gallows' rights, no one regretted the disappearance of a relic of medieval civil government, and the system of sheriff courts was extended and strengthened by the appointment of more sheriff deputes. Attempts to fasten the English system of justices of the peace had long been made in Scotland, but never worked well in conjunction with heritable jurisdictions, nor did J Ps show much zeal in this role in the following decades. Drawn from the same ranks of heritors, the ruling classes continued to manage country districts through the prevailing deference shown to property owners; the police force was negligible.

Hogarth saw this exiled Jacobite in France in 1761

The forfeited estates

Only in the Highlands were law and order enforced by military occupation. Fort George was built slowly, in the years after the last Rising, to replace the lost castle of Inverness blown up by the Jacobites, and to overawe the Great Glen. It is a superb statement of Georgian military and civil confidence, and the finest complex of buildings of the age in the north, with strong defences walling in vast parade grounds, barracks and magazines, and the royal arms prominently displaying the white horse of Hanover over the main gateway. Fort George was militarily obsolete before it was finished in the 1760s, but its effectiveness as a symbol of authority, and as a permanent base for troops, was unquestionable. The other Hanoverian forts were also garrisoned until all fear of a Jacobite resurgence was over.

The formation in 1754 of the Commissioners for Forfeited and Annexed Estates under the Barons of the Exchequer legalized the appropriation of about thirty estates belonging to former rebels. Thirteen were not only forfeited to the crown, but were annexed 'in perpetuity'. The number of estates was comparatively small, as many had managed to retain their lands by sitting at home while younger brothers or sons went out for the prince. The Duke of Atholl had prudently gone to take the waters in Bath in 1745, while his brother Lord George Murray had become the Jacobite chief of staff. However, the estates administered by the crown were extensive, and in the north-west were poor and primitive in organization. The brief of the commissioners was contradictory: they were to show the benighted tenantry that the rule of King George was more benevolent than their erstwhile owners' had been, and were to employ the most modern methods of improved agriculture, also introducing industry, fishing and mining to encourage progress in the Highlands and to reconcile the inhabitants with the benign Whig administration enjoyed by the rest of Britain.

The commissioners themselves, those who bothered to attend the meetings in Edinburgh, were enlightened landowners, improving farmers and legal luminaries of impeccable Whig background, and they strove to implement this brief. Factors, of Lowland and military background, were sent out to the estates, and for years laboured to improve them. Admirable maps were made by Peter May and other distinguished surveyors, meticulously listing ground under headings of improvable, waste, and unimprovable. A mineral expert was called in and tramped the Highlands; unfortunately he could only find a little coal at Brora in Sutherland. The linen industry was encouraged by bounties, and the leasing of plant to linen factors from Perth and other centres. The great wheel was introduced, to improve the quality of domestic spinning, and spinning schools were subsidized. Soldiers and sailors returning from colonial wars were given grants of land and a minimum of tools and capital to colonize remote areas. Mills were built, lime kilns opened.

Unfortunately these excellent projects largely failed, as the tenantry were quick to take advantage of the crucial clause emphasizing the benevolence of the crown.

No evictions, tough regulation, or wholesale reorganization of the tiny scattered holdings of the tenantry were possible, though reorganization was seen to be essential. Those who were threatened with change had their vigorous protests upheld. The soldiers' settlements did not flourish, the new plantations of timber were taken for firewood or grazed by cattle; in general the tenants ran rings round the factors, while longing for the return of their old unregenerate landlords. Some improvement there undoubtedly was, though whether it would have come faster or slower without the commissioners is debatable. 'We have succeeded in building a number of white houses in Coigach,' reported one factor, as he replaced a few black houses of thatch and rough stone with mortared, lime-washed and slated houses containing a fireplace and chimney. Many black houses remained.

After a generation most of the forfeited estates were returned to family ownership, and the annexed estates remained to be considered. Zeal for administering them had cooled, and by 1784 the last of them were recovered by the families of the former rebels, who had to pay handsomely for this privilege, and otherwise show their loyalty to King George. An effective way to do this was to raise a regiment for service in the colonial wars. Highland regiments had been formed since the days of Wade and the Black Watch, but the heyday of recruitment came with the wars of the second half of the eighteenth century. Simon Fraser recovered the Lovat estates of his kinsman as a reward for raising a regiment that fought at Quebec with Wolfe; Lord MacLeod recovered the Cromartie estates after raising two battalions of foot from the tenantry of his father's annexed estates and taking them to fight in India in 1780.

Clearances and other solutions

The industrial revolution, which was bringing work and real, if uneven, prosperity to the Clyde and Central Scotland and to the good farmlands of the country, had an adverse effect on the fringe lands: the Borders and the north, the west and the Hebrides. The old self-sufficient townships with lands farmed in common were becoming economically distressed by the late eighteenth century as customs changed, and landlords demanded increasing cash rents. A poet in the household of the Maclean chief made the point neatly in a Gaelic poem of the mid-eighteenth century:

> What has brought you these new debts
> is your liking for the Lowlands,
> the little pot[1] beside the hearth
> with the honey-tasting brew in it,
> spending what your father used
> to keep an armed household.
>
> Iain Mac Ailein

[1] a tea pot

None of this development solved Highland agricultural and industrial dilemmas. The ground was still poor, peaty and acid, unsuitable for arable crops, and by the end of the century the heavy increases in population put greater pressures on it, compounded by the arrival of the potato which supported more people on less land. Various solutions were put forward by landowners. Some such as the chief of Grant went in for improvement farms on a small scale of fifty acres or so, and for subsidies of lime and better seed. These improvers were a minority, and needed capital to back their improvements: in Grant's case this was supplied by the sale of timber from the forests of Spey. Mackenzie of Coull was a writer and advocate of enclosure, Clydesdale horsepower and large-scale improvement farms in Easter Ross, which had long been an arable area, and was suitable for enclosure on the Lothian scale. The dispossessed of Easter Ross went to farm in Orkney in their old primitive ways.

Owners of large mountainous estates, however, had a worse problem, and greeted the extension of sheep farming with enthusiasm. The growing markets of industrial towns offered a sure opening for meat and wool, it was argued, better than the sale of small black cattle, whose price anyhow dropped after the Napoleonic wars. Enclosure of large tracts of land, and the building of sheep farms, entailed the eviction of the resident population of the estates. In the classic case of the Sutherland estates, great care was given to resettling the tenantry in new coastal towns, where it was expected they would turn their attentions to herring fishing and kelp-gathering. Most of these coastal towns were expensive failures.

Evictions in the Highlands and elsewhere in Britain were backed by due processes of law, and the sheriff's officer and armed men frequently attended to ensure that the tenants complied with eviction notices. The ministers preached

compliance with the will of the landlord. Sadly in the Highlands the tenantry had no desire for change and had an intense sense of belonging to their land and loyalty to their hereditary landlord. The sense of betrayal and shock was enormous, and the scale and ruthlessness of the clearances was great. Between the Year of the Sheep (1792), and the early years of Victoria great areas of the north were cleared of men and given over to black-faced sheep.

> Not sweet the sound that waked me from slumber
> coming down to me from the mountain tops:
> the Lowland shepherd whose tongue displeases,
> shouting there at his lazy dog . . .
>
> Iain MacLachlainn

Emigration

Emigration was no new solution, there had been mass movements from Skye and the mainland in the 1770s, years of famine and distress in the north, together with an upward spiral of rents. Dr Johnson, one of the first romantic English travellers to the north, witnessed the weeping departure of many on one boat bound to the Carolinas. Emigration greatly increased during the clearances, with families leaving the little black houses of their ancestors for the unknown world of Canada, the Americas or Australia. Individual families often followed an adventurous forerunner, establishing little enclaves, often called after their homeland. Shipping agents often enticed emigrants with promises of new lands to be reached by payment of very cheap fares: the conditions on these ships were, however, atrocious and the new lands hard to break in. Some tacksmen presided over a mass movement of their tenants: a Mackenzie of Kilcoy in the Black Isle accompanied a shipload of his people, with schoolmaster and piper, to a new settlement near Moreton Bay in Queensland (he spent the voyage learning Gaelic) but that was exceptional.

Most went reluctantly, and the very old and very young often died on the way. Others emigrated from the Highlands as far as the new Lowland industrial towns, where they formed distinct communities, and often followed the same trade. By the nineteenth century seasonal migration was an accepted part of Highland life for those who were left. Summer labourers went out to bring in Lowland harvests, and the fisher-lassies followed the herring fleets around Britain, gutting and packing fish. There was little prospect of a good living at home, and many men joined the army and navy, further draining the glens of manpower.

Crofting

A common fate, and the one now enshrined in the popular mind, was forcible resettlement from inland townships into small crofts on marginal land, on heights or coastlands where it was intended that the crofter would learn 'to fish, or to burn kelp to supply an early industrial need for alkali. (The kelp market boomed during the Napoleonic wars and collapsed soon afterwards; fortunes had been made, but not by the kelp-burners.) Crofting was a development of the late eighteenth century and gave an inadequate marginal living, almost wholly dependent on the potato crop. Crofting allowed those who clung to the land to remain in Highland parishes; crofting rents were too high for such tenants to pay and too low to offer an attractive return, or any margin for improvement to landlords, even the well-intentioned. Crofting contributed to the stagnation of economic life in the Highlands.

The worst proprietors, those least concerned with the welfare or even the whereabouts of their displaced tenants, appear to have been widow ladies, holding lands in trust for minor sons in whose names some ruthless evictions were undertaken in Chisholm country, Glengarry and elsewhere. The sheepwalks never provided an adequate return either. Overproduction of coarse wool and cheap mutton did not make fortunes. Among all the gainers from the industrial revolution in Britain there were some losers: the Scots, Irish and Welsh who lived on mountains or on marginal peat lands, for whom no new role could be found.

XI
Up to Victoria

The Statistical Account

SIR JOHN SINCLAIR of Ulbster stood up in the General Assembly of the Church of Scotland in 1790 to propose that all ministers should be sent a questionnaire on the state of their parishes. Sinclair proposed to coordinate the replies himself and was wealthy enough to be able largely to finance the enterprise. Statistics were in vogue, and the need to provide a comprehensive picture of Britain had been discussed before this date; the first national census followed in 1801. Sinclair had the determination and the status to see his project through. By 1791 the first of the 21 volumes of the *Old Statistical Account* was published, to be followed by the rest, up to the laggard returns of 1797.

One hundred and sixty-six questions were asked, of 900 ministers. Naturally their essays in reply show almost as many variations and cannot be neatly tabulated. The questions concerned population, and changes noted; land under cultivation and crops grown, the work of the people—almost exclusively agricultural—and details of wages, new industries and incidence of unemployment. Food and fuel prices were requested, and notes on the history and natural history of the parish. According to taste and intellect, the replies concentrate on one or other aspect; some ministers are full of the beauties and historic associations of their area, or of the great names among their heritors; others go into practical details of how a farm labourer can manage on an annual wage of about £15 when his annual expenditure is in the order of £17.14s.4d—the shortfall was made up by his wife doing casual farm labour at harvest time. Many were concerned at the price of coal, but commented on how its recent introduction by sea over a wide area of Scotland had improved a situation becoming difficult as peat bogs were worked out. The minister of Cromarty in Ross was one of these.

The accounts in all their variety conjure up pictures of candlelit manse studies and diligent men, Moderates for the most, penning with some pride and a little complacency the account of their parish. 'There are no Papists' is a fairly frequent entry. Many give detailed accounts of the improvements undertaken by an enlightened landlord, such as the laird of Glen Urquhart with his free lime and free seeds; his workers, however, only received the Highland average wage of £12 per annum. In the parishes which had experienced most expansion a note of doubt and wonderment occasionally creeps in. The children who work in cotton-spinning mills are difficult to educate, the poor of expanding parishes are difficult to provide for. In Kirkintilloch, just outside Glasgow, many changes had recently taken place, and the farmers had nearly all gone over to dairying, in consequence of the cutting of the Forth-Clyde canal, which enabled them to send milk to Glasgow by boat, and to retrieve the empty churns. The discursive pages of the *Old Statistical Account* are full of such touches, and give an unrivalled picture of Scotland in a process of transition from the eighteenth to the nineteenth centuries. Both continuity and change were in the air.

Politics: The French Revolution and war

In 1789 the French Revolution gathered momentum, stimulating great public interest. More newspapers were printed and circulated in Scotland, and there were various minor results. Women's fashions suddenly changed from the wearing of heavy silks to the clinging muslins of Liberty; hairdressing for both sexes meant short classic locks, no more wigs or powder. Burns (whose career we shall soon come to) wore his hair *à la Brutus*, and wrote of the early stage of the Revolution with passion:

> Heard ye o' the Tree o' France
> I watna what's the name o't;
> Around it a' the patriots dance
> Weel Europe kens the fame o't;
> It stands where ance the Bastille stood . . .

For all this superficial interest and visual change, the government of Scotland was tightly in the hands of Henry Dundas of Arniston, a Lothian laird and lawyer-politician who, by epitomizing the consensus, was able to control the country in a way that was endorsed by nearly every member of the traditional ruling classes, and only questioned by a tiny radical minority. Dundas was closely allied to William Pitt the Younger, the Prime Minister, who had spent a short time at Glasgow University in his teens. Dundas, in addition to managing Scotland, was long a member and finally President of the Board of Control of the East India Company. These interests worked together. Dundas's access to almost limitless patronage in India as well as at home gave him control of virtually all the aspiring Scots, whose road to achievement outside Scotland lay through his 'machine'. In the general election of 1790 it was reckoned that 34 out of the 45 Scottish MPs belonged to the Dundas interest; many Scottish seats were not even contested.

Public feelings were satisfied by enthusiasm for the war, for the formation and drilling of volunteer and fencible regiments all over the country, and less enthusiastically for the militia, a form of compulsory military service introduced in 1797. Places in the ranks were decided by ballot, and it was easy enough for well-connected young men to find a substitute. It was harder for young artisans to avoid call-up and militia service was much resented, to the point of riot in Tranent, an East Lothian mining centre, and in other Fife and Lowland areas. Recruitment to the regular army was greatly stepped up, and the formation by Wellington of a Highland brigade to fight in the Peninsular War brought Highland fighting men into public prominence.

The number of Scotsmen who actively opposed the government and supported French ideals was small, and not as well organized as the contemporary United Irishmen. In 1792 the first Friends of the People societies were formed in Edinburgh and Glasgow. The Edinburgh society was actively promoted by a young advocate, Thomas Muir of Huntershill, who became vice president, one of several gentry who were not afraid to advocate changes following the French example. He unwisely read out to the society a message from the United Irishmen which was too violent for Scottish tastes, alarmed anyway by a commendation from the Committee of Public Safety in France itself. After a visit to Paris at the time of the king's execution, Muir returned to Scotland to stand his trial. He was arrested and sentenced to transportation, after a travesty of a trial. His name is said to be the only one ever expunged from the roll of advocates.

After the trial the Glasgow radicals became more active as United Scotsmen. Citoyen Mengaud, the French secret envoy to Scotland, reported that the Scots were much disposed to revolution, and that this feeling had existed since the union. A futile expedition was launched by France, to aid the Irish and Scots conspirators, but it was defeated easily when it made a landing at Fishguard in Wales and the local fencibles were alerted. Even the United Scotsmen were relieved, but annoyed with such misdirected French aid. The government continued to suppress the United Scotsmen whose meetings were secret, but often infiltrated by government spies and reporters, and their fire died down to embers. Muir escaped from Australia and after vicissitudes arrived in France where he died in 1799, aged 33. He was the only real leader among the Scottish underground. His mother wrote of his early death:

> And all for sowing with a liberal hand,
> The seeds of that seditious libel—Truth.

The India connection: 'Scotland's corn kist'

India gave an opening for advancement to many Scots, though the heavy mortality there also made for many graves: 'Two monsoons is the life of a man.' In 1784 Pitt's India Act recognized that servants of the Honourable Company had to govern huge tracts of territory as well as administer India's trade. In 1784 Highland regiments wearing the king's uniform were engaged in extending this territory in southern India. The rampant corruption of Clive's previous generation of Company servants was followed by more control and less rapacity, though fortunes could still be made quickly by survivors of the murderous climate and the resolutely British lifestyle they adhered to in India. General Claud Alexander is a good example; he returned to Scotland in about 1785, after reforms were instituted, and he invested the fortune made during his service as Paymaster-General in Bengal in a new cotton mill at Catrine, one of the Arkwright models, on the advice of and in partnership with his banker David Dale. John Galt's *Annals of the Parish* gives a thinly fictionalized account of Alexander and the coming of cotton to a remote Ayrshire parish.

A more important, and in some ways more characteristic figure who went from Scotland to India to find fortune, was Charles Grant of Shewglie in Glen Urquhart. He was born near Inverness in March 1746, named for Prince Charles and christened under the drawn claymore of his father and 30 friends 'out for the Prince', on the eve of Culloden. It was an unpromising start to any career. His father hid after the battle, then went to the West Indies where he died of fever, leaving Mistress Grant with five small children. Shewglie had been burnt by order of Cumberland's troops, and the family were impoverished. Charles, however, was sent to a good school in Elgin, as the importance of education was fully grasped. At 13 he was apprenticed to an uncle who had a fish factoring business in Cromarty, and learned business method in his counting house. Another relative found him a clerkship in an India merchant's counting house in London, and after five years there he went to India without an appointment, which was technically illegal, and made himself indispensable to a Company officer, Becher, as private secretary. Becher was Resident in Murshidabad, Bengal, at a time of acute famine; he hadn't a very savoury reputation. Grant returned after two years, able to travel in the first chaise ever seen in Glen Urquhart, and to endow his two sisters with dowries of £300 each, which he hoped would be sufficient to offset their plain countenances. In London he was able, through the Becher connection, to obtain the desired qualification as a Writer to the Company, and to return to India legitimately. He took with him a Highland bride.

When Grant and his wife arrived in Calcutta in 1773 they were greeted by a brother of Grant's in the Company's Marine Service, and two cousins; soon they were joined by another brother and Mrs Grant's mother and sister. India was indeed full of Scots. Grant spent more than ten years in Bengal, acquiring useful experience in the Board of Trade for Bengal, and in a silk factory. He lived extravagantly and was in debt until the tragic deaths of two daughters from smallpox brought him and his wife to a sudden Christian conversion. From thenceforward they lived in terms of extreme evangelical piety, and in revulsion to luxury though not to comfort. In Calcutta Grant fostered an illegal church; the Company's policy was resolutely against such interference in native customs, especially in native religions. Grant rejected this attitude. He began corresponding with Wilberforce and other leading English Evangelicals, though not apparently with any Scots. He left Bengal in 1790, with a useful number of influential friends from Lord Cornwallis downwards.

On return to Britain Grant settled in Clapham with neighbours who shared his outlook and of whom Wilberforce was the best known. The only other Scotsman was Zaccariah Macaulay, a powerful Evangelical from Stornoway. Grant made occasional short autumn visits to Inverness-shire. He was gratified to be consulted secretly by Pitt and Dundas on Indian affairs. The abolition of slavery was the great Evangelical cause, seconded by the opening of British Indian territories to missionaries; Pitt and Dundas, however, were more interested in the renewal of the Company's charter in 1793. This was achieved without change in any direction, in spite of evangelical pleading on one hand, and the pressure just being brought by the outport merchants, including those of Glasgow, for free trade and the ending of monopoly.

Grant became a member of the Court of Directors of the Company and, by the next renewal of the charter in 1813, was President. He stood firm for missions, and against free trade. Titanic battles raged, in a pamphlet war and in parliamentary debate, and in the pages of the great Edinburgh magazines, then at the height of their influence. Grant argued his case for the *status quo ante* in Indian trade at great length. He had been elected as Member of Parliament for Inverness-shire in 1801, but sat as leader of the Indian interest; Dundas gave him his blessing, but Lovat, the sitting Member then out of favour, contested the seat. The voting figures for the largest county in the British Isles give the claustrophobic narrowness of the franchise:

Grant 15   Lovat 11   Forbes of Culloden 6

Grant continued to represent Inverness-shire, and eventually his sons Charles and Robert represented Elgin Burghs, and Inverness Burgh. The 1813 charter of the East India Company was victory and a defeat for Grant, missionaries received the right of entry to Company territories, but so did the dreaded free traders. Grant died in 1823, when he had become a relic of a bygone age. Pitt had fallen over the issue of Catholic emancipation, and had died young in 1806; Dundas had been disgraced over a fairly trivial piece of jobbery over naval estimates and had died in 1811; and Kirkman Finlay and other Glasgow merchants were sending regular sailings from the Clyde to Calcutta and Bombay, where their young agents were forming chambers of commerce on the Glasgow pattern, in the teeth of Company hostility.

Grant is an instructive example of the successful Scotsman of his day: once he was established he virtually turned his back on his country. He bought a property in Inverness-shire, Waternish on the Isle of Skye, to qualify as a Member of Parliament, but he did not visit it for ten years, and then only for a day when he found, not surprisingly, that the situation of the tenants was 'melancholy'. He dispensed patronage to a further generation of Scotsmen who served in India and was generous to his family, but never seems to have wanted to leave London and the charmed circle of Leadenhall Street and Clapham. He was buried in St George's, Bloomsbury, where the Company paid for a handsome marble tablet; if he had retained much of Highland sentiment he would have insisted that his bones were returned to Glen Urquhart.

The abolition of slavery was an issue in which Scottish opinion did lead the rest of Britain. The men of the Enlightenment, going back to Hutcheson at the beginning of the century, were the first to make hostile references to the practice. However, it was the Reverend James Ramsay, an Episcopalian from Peterhead who spent 18 years as a chaplain in the West Indies, who wrote and preached most vigorously against both slavery and the slave trade. He had irrefutable first-hand evidence. He returned to Britain in 1784 and was taken up by Professor Beattie of Aberdeen. Beattie, besides providing his students with the useful list of avoidable *Scotticisms*, wrote a prosy but popular *Essay . . . on Truth*, before throwing himself into anti-slavery work in 1790. Ramsay and Beattie formed the attitudes and provided the weapons for the reformers. The slave trade was abolished in 1807, and slavery in the British domains in 1837.

Burns and Scott: the literary giants

Robert Burns's (1759-96) reputation as a poet has lasted and has grown. His influence has been deep, but different facets of his work have attracted admiration in different generations. In his life he was hailed as a prodigy, a 'ploughman poet' (though there were many who made verses in rural areas). Some ill-advised friends in Edinburgh tried to patronize him and induce him to polish his work and make it more English. Fortunately he soon gave up the unprofitable attempt and continued to write in the spoken language of Scotland. He drew on the great store of ballads and songs still alive in his day; like Scott later, he collected them and in some cases rewrote them. Burns was able to identify with the strong old roots of the oral tradition, especially that of the Mearns from which his family came, and he could make poetry of the problems and pleasures of being young and hard-up in Ayrshire in the 1770s. To read Burns's *Epistles* to his friends is to overhear the authentic voice of rural Scotland, educated, shrewd, opinionated and quite uncowed by authority, robust in pleasure and concerned with relationships of God and man. When he ploughed up a mouse's nest on the hard upland farm of Mossgiel he wrote a parable for poor labourers, evicted by forces outside their control. Improved farming had losers as well as winners in the late eighteenth century:

> Thou saw the fields laid bare an' wast,
> An' weary winter comin fast,
> An' cozie here, beneath the blast
>   Thou thought to dwell
> Till crash! the cruel coulter past
>   Out thro' thy cell

Burns Nights throughout the world, wherever exiled Scots gather, have often become an easy sentimental exercise in mass nostalgia. Burns himself was compassionate, tough and entirely worthy of respect.

Walter Scott was the most influential Scotsman of his age. He coloured the outlook of several generations of Scots, and moulded the outlook of Europeans in general on Scotland; his influence can in some ways still be felt. He was born in 1771 and mixed with Edinburgh legal circles, just at the time that polite society was beginning to romanticize the vanishing world of the Highlands. Jacobite songs were returning to drawing rooms, and many of them which have become standard were newly written at this point, by Caroline Lady Nairne, of an old Perthshire Jacobite family. It may have been part of the late eighteenth-century preoccupation with a vanishing pastoral scene, romanticizing the Highlander as Marie Antoinette was romanticizing milkmaids, now that the threat had gone.

Scott trained for the law and became an advocate. He had been stirred by the publishing of Percy's *Reliques*, and had collaborated with the publisher Ballantyne to publish three volumes of *Border Minstrelsy* in 1802-3. Scott had collected much of the material, reworked a good deal and set his collection firmly in the English-Scottish Border territory. This was distortion of evidence; one of his best sources had been an old lady in Falkland, Fife, who had the ballads from her mother, and came from the true Highland/Lowland border country of the Mearns, Burns's ancestral land. After this success he turned his own talent to verse, and published rapidly a number of long romantic poems of which 'The Lay of the Last Minstrel', 'Marmion' and 'The Lady of the Lake' are the best known. They were an instant success, and their popularity laid the foundations of the Scottish tourist trade, particularly in the Trossachs, where 'The Lady of the Lake' was set. Scott himself never travelled much in Scotland, not, it is thought, much north of Perth, except for a foray to Shetland by sea, so his Highland settings lack a little conviction, though they have much enthusiasm.

He turned to fiction, and published *Waverley* anonymously in 1814; subsequent novels were 'by the author of *Waverley*' and the secret was not disclosed for 13 years. Scott found his true genius in writing novels. *Waverley* embodies every romantic attitude towards the Highlanders and the rising of 1745 subsequently cherished by every Lowland and English reader; it coloured the imagination of generations. Scott achieved a balance in his novels by presenting a central, usually rather neutral, character who stands between two extremes of thought and action. His finest work was *Heart of Midlothian*, published early in the series in 1818. In it Scott achieved his greatest imaginative reconstruction of the stresses of life in Scotland after the union. The long, peculiarly Scottish conflict of conscience between duty to God and duty to the state underpins an exciting and thickly populated narrative. *Heart of Midlothian* is a masterpiece. Scott and his partner and publisher Ballantyne overreached themselves and became heavily in debt, a debt which Scott compounded by building a Border baronial hall for himself at Abbotsford, where he lived out his dreams. In 1826 the joint business went bankrupt, and Scott wrote himself to death in an honourable effort to pay off the large sums involved, dying in 1832.

The influence of Scott on every facet of Scottish life cannot be measured. For example in architecture a romantic gothic took the place of severe classic lines. The nobility, whose ancestors had carefully modernized their ancient keeps, under Scott's influence restored the battlements, pepper-pot towers, chimneys and gables of baronial halls: pepper pots also sprouted along the skylines of suburban roads, where manufacturers lived in new comfort. Civic fathers tore down old town houses to rebuild in Scottish baronial style, as happened in Inverness. The fashion in Scots baronial building culminated at Balmoral.

The Tartan Review

Among Scott's enthusiastic readers were the Prince Regent, and the future Queen Victoria. When the Regent became King George IV he decided to be the first Hanoverian monarch to visit Scotland—the first king since Charles II, as he was proud to relate. He commanded Walter Scott to organize the royal visit.

The Tartan Review

Scott's authorship was by this time the worst-kept secret in the north. He set about the royal visit with enthusiasm. The Tartan Review, as it came to be called, of 1822 was a notable landmark. The king had commanded all his loyal chiefs to attend wearing their Highland dress. This put a number of gentlemen, more used to taking their dress from the prince's own English example or from that of his friend Brummel, into states of anxiety and embarrassment. Only the military had retained the Highland garb, and had developed it into a version of their own. The chiefs had to fall back on misty recollections and the fragments of authentic tartan that family piety had preserved through the long years of the Disarming Act. Whig families had less difficulty than the Jacobite survivors. Those who had no tartan were forced back on the services offered by Messrs Wilson of Bannockburn, a wool-spinning mill with the finest hand-weavers of central Scotland on their books. Wilsons reconstructed, or in some cases designed, clan tartans for all the major Scottish chiefs. In the case of the two leading 'imperialist' clans, Campbell and Mackenzie, the chosen tartans were modifications of the Government Sett, worn by the Black Watch. Weapon-makers and jewellers also worked hard to provide authentic equipment.

When George IV landed at Leith from the royal yacht he was greeted by crowded tiers of loyal subjects, the Company of Archers drawn up in full uniform, and Walter Scott as master of ceremonies. All were gratified to behold that the monarch was clad in full Highland dress himself, and was accompanied by his old friend the Lord Mayor of London, similarly garbed. They had both taken the precaution of wearing pink tights under the unaccustomed kilt.

The king held a Drawing Room at which young ladies were presented by their mamas, and a banquet at Holyroodhouse. There the Loyal Toast was proposed by the chief of clan MacGregor, descendant of the clan most hounded for knavery and Jacobite plotting by earlier monarchs. MacGregor made a speech of fulsome loyalty which was acknowledged in the gracious reply. Later the chief had his portrait painted by Raeburn, in all the glory of his eagle-feathered bonnet, as did McNab and Glengarry. The Tartan Review was a triumph for Scott's romantic view of Scotland's past, and has given rise to a century and a half of subsequent posturing and piping. Wilsons of Bannockburn extended their mills, installed power weaving, and had a booming business based on exports of tartan to Europe and America.

The New Statistical Account

By the end of the 1830s it was felt in the General Assembly of the Church of Scotland that the original *Statistical Account* of 40 years before was quite outdated, and a new compilation was undertaken. A comparison between the *Old Statistical Account* of 1790-7 and the *New Statistical Account*, published in the early 1840s, does show the great changes which had come to the land. The minister of Alloa, an old coal-mining centre, remarked somewhat complacently that the new steam railway which was expected to come to Alloa from Stirling shortly after he had made his report was the seventh railway to be built in the neighbourhood: he described the various railways of wooden beams and man- or horse-drawn waggons which had conveyed coal from the pithead to the staithes and quays of the port since the mid-seventeenth century. That minister was aware of progression. Many others displayed either naïve wonder at the new marvels of technology, or bewilderment that the great shifts in population had utterly altered the old patterns and the old values of Scotland. Many showed awareness that the education of children in the new industrial towns had declined sharply from its previous good level; working children could not be expected to make good scholars, nor was much opportunity given them. The terrible cholera epidemic of 1831-2 receives occasional mention. The ministers of the *New Statistical Account* do not present the coherent front which the Moderate men of the earlier generation had done; they are a prey to doubts and questionings, or bland disregard of startling change. All of them were on the eve of the last convulsion in the religious life of the country, the Disruption. But before we look at this very Scottish happening there are a few other points to note.

The integration of Scotland into the larger whole of Great Britain was speeded by two events of the early nineteenth century: the increasing pace of industrialization, and the reform of political life after the Reform Bill of 1832. Industrialization was so much a countrywide phenomenon that it has few specifically Scottish aspects. Cotton spinning and weaving kept pace with developments in Lancashire; shipbuilding was mirrored in Tyneside and Belfast, trade with India was closely matched with Liverpool's. Labour movements tended to derive from English patterns, though curiously the early trade unionists of Scotland did not show the same militancy as their English counterparts. Chartism was never very strong in Scotland, and employers managed to keep wages at lower levels than in comparable English industries. One manufacturer said smugly to a royal commission on conditions in cotton mills that this was because the Scottish workers were more thrifty, and lived on oatmeal which was cheaper than wheat bread. They were, he declared, healthier and better off than English workers. For all that, the conditions of mill workers, children, and women in mines were explored by several parliamentary commissions, whose ultimate inspiration had been the statistical and utilitarian approach of teachers in the University of Edinburgh.

One of the most significant of these commissions was Edwin Chadwick's *Report on the Sanitary Condition of the Labouring Population of Great Britain.* This was presented to Parliament in 1842. Compilation of the Scottish section of the report had been hampered by the lack of Poor Law registration and civil registration in Scotland, leaving little statistical basis. However, this lack was compensated by the enthusiasm with which unofficial sources responded to Chadwick's request for information. The Edinburgh medical school had 'long radiated enthusiasms for public health reform' and was led by Dr William Allison, who had himself attacked urban squalor in his *Observations on the Poor Law in Scotland.* In Glasgow Dr Cleland, the Burgh Medical Officer of Health, had long been a campaigner for beter information and better care; the Professor of Forensic Medicine in Glasgow, Robert Cowan, proved a powerful ally for Chadwick.

The picture these informants and others built up was a disgraceful one of urban filth and municipal neglect. Crowded tenements without piped water bred typhus and tick-borne fevers, and epidemic cholera swept through them (and on into the houses of the clean well-to-do). Tuberculosis was endemic. Babies died. In Stirling the lack of public drainage was held up to view: there were no water pipes or sewage pipes below ground. The drains of the castle, the town jail and a flourishing butchery ran down the steep cobbles through the whole length of the town on different days in the week. The basements of the old town houses of the nobility of Scotland, at the top of the town, were used as middens and receptacles for rubbish. In Dundee the water supply was taxed by the great demand made by steam engines in the manufactories: water was condensed and reused many times. Flax spinning, Dundee's great industry at this time, demanded a great deal of water for the purpose of spinning in a mist of water vapour. The permanent dampness of the young operatives led, it was considered, to weakness and disease.

Chadwick's report stirred the civic conscience of Scottish burghs. These had only just been reformed; the legislation which had reformed the English boroughs and had made policing, lighting and cleansing matters for civic concern in England had been delayed until the implementation of the Scottish Police Acts in the 1840s. Chadwick's report, together with the great public alarm which the cholera epidemic of 1831-2 had occasioned, was the beginning of a general concern with drainage, fresh water supply and medical care. All over Britain it was noticeable that Chadwick's vanguard of informers and campaigners for public health were the medical men trained in the schools of Edinburgh and Glasgow. However, Chadwick's report, which covered the whole of Great Britain, emphasizes that Britain had become integrated by the mid-century.

Reform

The end of the Napoleonic wars brought little reassurance to the rulers of Britain, who feared radical agitation more than they feared Napoleon. A deep economic depression was the aftermath of war. In the Highlands and Islands the fall in kelp prices, due to imports and new synthetic chemicals, was coupled with an intense period of eviction and clearance, as landlords faced their debts. Emigration increased. The fall in black cattle prices, after war profiteering ceased, also affected rural economies. As severe was the distress in the towns, where textiles were in a slump; agitation against the revised Corn Law of 1815 revealed the deep and growing divergence of interest between the land (including tenant farmers) and the industrialists and working classes of the towns. Protection for the landed meant privation for town dwellers, or so it was widely believed. The Scots Poor Law was overstrained and inadequate, and the authorities had some justification for their fears of a radical rising. None really developed.

In spite of the harsh Combination Laws some artisans managed to form secret societies and unions, particularly in the mines and among textile workers. Few of these advocated direct action—self-improvement and self-education were the road preferred by Scottish artisans. There were few home-grown leaders at this time, and the radical Scots looked to the initiative of Englishmen, particularly to the well-thumbed writings of Tom Paine and Cobbett and to the speeches made by the elderly Major Cartwright, who toured Scotland in 1815, promoting demands for such things as an annual Parliament, a secret ballot, and salaries for MPs. It was clearly seen on all sides that these demands would loosen the control of the landed interest.

In 1820 for a short time it looked as if the fears of the government were going to be realized, as agitation grew in the west of Scotland. Embittered by the Peterloo massacre of peaceful demonstrators in Manchester the previous year, and by repressive measures in Paisley and Greenock, a handful of weavers formed an army, less than 40 strong, and marched on the Carron Iron Works to capture arms. They were easily dispersed near Bonnybridge by armed troops, and three of them were hanged.

Whig and Tory—new style

The old alignments between Whig and Tory underwent a shift throughout Britain. In Scottish terms, Tory had been the half-affectionate description either of an antiquated Jacobite, or a country gentleman of traditional mould. Pitt's Tory administration changed that, and gave the country a broader policy which in wartime found wide acceptance. This was the party of Dundas in Scotland, and it was unchallenged for many years. After his eclipse an alternative emerged from the debating clubs of Edinburgh, the new-style Whig party, composed of liberal young men. They used the old label of Whig, associated with Argyll and the Williamites, though it is doubtful if Islay would have endorsed the faintest radical notion. By 1829 the long-simmering problem of the legal disabilities of Catholics in Great Britain had developed into crisis, with the debate and passing of the Catholic Emancipation Bill. This shocked those of traditional outlook who believed that the very existence of the state was bound up with the Protestant Settlement, of whom there were many in Scotland.

The Reform Bill in Scotland

Agitation for the reform of Parliament had had just such a long history as Catholic emancipation, and the pressures mounted, convincing the Tory party that reform was safe, stabilizing and desirable. It was in fact introduced by a new Whig administration in 1832. Scotland had a separate Bill, following the Reform Act of England and Wales, extending the franchise to owners of property worth £10 per annum, and reallocating the burgh seats to give representation to such cities as Falkirk and Paisley which had grown great, but were not royal burghs of the old dispensation. The property qualification for voting broke the stranglehold over burgh representation that had been held by the burgh councils.

159

The voting strength of Scotland was increased from a total of just over four thousand to sixty-five thousand. But without secret ballot, and with a lack of adequate definition over who was worth ten pounds, it was soon seen that a good deal of old-fashioned manipulation was still possible, and the change in Scottish politics was not dramatic. The burghs on the whole were Whiggish, and the county seats returned Tories from old landed families, as they had always done. Following the reform of Parliament and the resultant shake-up of burgh administration a number of other measures were passed rather slowly through Parliament in the wake of English legislation. Acts for the setting up of commissions for police enabled towns to pave, light and clean their streets, as well as to police them in the interests of law and order, and water supplies became a civic concern. The Whigs congratulated one another on reforms so far reaching as to be final, and Tories in the mould of Sir Walter Scott predicted the ruin of the country.

The Disruption of 1843

The last wholly Scottish event with which this volume deals is the Disruption of the kirk, which took place in 1843. It was the most recent manifestation of the old struggle between the church and the state, and had been a long time in coming to a head. In 1712 the Patronage Act had restored to heritors the right of presentation to parishes and this, although it suited the deferential temper of the day, was the cause of the deep unrest in those few parishes which clung to the old right of election of the minister by the elders, and the right to veto any minister intruded on them against their will. Galt's *Annals of the Parish* carries an entertaining account of the intrusion of a minister.

By the end of the century Moderate ministers were beginning to have to take note of the rival Evangelicals. These were misleadingly named, as their views did not coincide with the English Evangelicals and Wesleyans, but were touched with the spirit most inimical to the age of reason: enthusiasm. In those days this was a term of criticism. The first of the secession churches broke away on the issue of patronage in the 1730s; it in turn fractured into two more components, which in turn split—the disestablished church seemed endlessly fissile. However, when more parishes became evangelical in outlook, towards the end of the eighteenth century, further secular complications were felt. The Moderate men were Whigs and traditionalists, upholders of the constitution and of the government—Dundas's government. The question asked was: were the Evangelicals to be equated with radicals or worse, Jacobins? No, they certainly were not, but they were mostly composed of those Scots whom the establishment most feared might become tinged with radicalism—the lower middle classes, the artisans and small tradesmen of the towns, particularly the new towns. Evangelicals campaigned for a reallocation of resources, to cope with the great new towns, where the working classes were seen to be quite uneducated, largely illiterate and indifferent to kirk debates, indeed quite indifferent to the kirk which had not been able to care for them. The working classes read Tom Paine and formed combinations to attack their grievances in wholly secular terms.

The Evangelicals came to be led by Thomas Chalmers, a dynamic preacher with a striking personality. In 1817 a volume of his sermons sold 20,000 copies. He became minister at the Tron Kirk in Glasgow, and gained deep experience of urban squalor and church commitment. His remedy was a return to the mythical golden age of the presbyterian past, when the rich assisted the poor through voluntary giving. Through his forceful personality he made this work for a few years in the Tron and St John's, Glasgow, but as a remedy for deep industrial poverty the voluntary giving of time and money by the rich was hopelessly idealistic, and inadequate; it faltered in times of industrial unrest and mutual hostility when aid was most needed.

The Poor Law of Scotland was under debate at the time, with the Scots rather smugly adhering to voluntary assessment and payment of relief by each parish under the benign auspices of its elders. The English Poor Laws relied on a statutory Poor Rate, and officers to dispense it. This system too had broken down, under the pressure of agricultural distress in England. Chalmers declared that

Nothing but the multiplication of our Established Churches with the sub-division of parishes . . . together with a pure and popular exercise of the right of patronage will ever bring us back again to a sound and wholesome state of the body politic [and] The proper remedy for the wretchedness of the few is the kindness of many.

The emphasis on the social duty of the church was fine as far as it went, but it disregarded the needs of the poor who were not members of the kirk: the dissenters, Episcopalians, and the increasing masses of Catholic Irish streaming into the new mining and ironworking towns of Lanarkshire.

For ten years the Evangelicals fought out issues of patronage in the Court of Session, an arid arena. Chalmers returned to his University of St Andrews where he influenced a whole generation of young ministers. The government resisted all petitions for dividing parishes, only conceding a measure in 1824 which proved a disappointment: the parishes to be divided were the remote Highland ones, not the teeming urban parishes. Money from the government for church building went into neat 'Parliamentary Kirks' designed by Thomas Telford in places as remote as Iona, not in new towns. The Evangelicals eventually gained the majority in the General Assembly, and raised a large sum of money for extension churchbuilding, only to be thwarted again by the government who would not make any provision for the new stipends required for the ministers to these kirks, nor give them legal recognition.

Open breach between the kirk and the state came early in 1843, when the Court of Session finally rejected an appeal over the congregation of Auchterarder's right to veto an undesired minister, and a Claim of Right was sent to Westminster, with complaints from the Assembly to both Houses arguing that the state had

invaded the rights of the church. The Kirk Assembly '. . . declare that they cannot in conscience carry on the government of Christ's Church subject to the coercion attempted by the Court of Session'. It was a brave declaration against the highest law court in the land; long memories stirred in Scotland. The Claim of Right was debated and rejected by Parliament with Brougham, a temperate Edinburgh Whig, declaring 'No well-governed country—no civilised authority—could exist if within its limits there was an authority greater than its laws.' The House rejected the Kirk's 'vain and extravagant claims'. For the next two months the whole of Scotland seethed with interest. The minister of Ferintosh, in Ross, preached on the text 'We ought to obey God rather than men', and other awkward texts were brought out. The government had to face strong subversive feeling on the part of those Scots who had hitherto been most dependable, the middle classes.

The Assembly, baffled by Parliament, approached the crown directly. The Assembly customarily exchanges a letter with the monarch early each year, in which loyal sentiments are expressed, and in return comes the nomination of a high commissioner who deputizes at the annual Assembly in the name of the monarch, in recognition of the kirk's established status. In 1843, to the horror of the court and government, a strongly-worded letter of protest was sent together with the loyal greetings to Queen Victoria. Her chilly reply took an uncompromising stand on the legal decision: 'The law . . . has confirmed that new parishes cannot be created by the authority of the church alone.' The Assembly trumped the royal reply by answering, 'On all these questions of most sacred interest it becomes us to invoke the aid of Divine Grace.' The Home Secretary wrote a fulminating reply to that, quoting Knox's *Book of Discipline*, every detail of which was reported and discussed in the Scottish newspapers and periodicals.

Chalmers and the Evangelicals were prepared to make any sacrifice except that of their principles. At the opening of the Assembly in May 1843 the Moderator,

Dr Welsh, declared that he in conscience could not regard it as a free assembly, and he left the building, followed by Chalmers and a great concourse of ministers. The final count was 451 ministers out of the total in all Scotland of 1024. They left the Established Church to form the disestablished Free Church of Scotland. Dr Candlish, one of the leaders, stated:

> I believe by God's blessing on our free and faithful preaching in the highways and hedges . . . we shall yet regenerate Scotland, and have multitudes of those who are now perishing for lack of Knowledge to listen to glad tidings.

They made a severe material sacrifice, leaving their snug manses and glebes and their stipends behind. However, for the government the moment of danger was past and what might have developed into a declaration of independence, had there been leaders more concerned with the underlying political implications than with religious ones, merely turned into the Disruption of the kirk, and not the rupture of the state.

About one third of the members of the Church of Scotland followed their ministers into the Free Kirk. In two years they had built nearly five hundred austere places of worship, and homes for the evicted ministers, had opened a theological training college and made provision for overseas mission. But the great principles of service to the underprivileged which had contributed so much to the Disruption were somehow lost, or were not harnessed to the urban areas as much as to remote Highland areas. The 'chiliasm (doctrine) of despair' found fertile ground in areas where Free Kirk ministers and people felt they must make a stand against the state, and at a local level the state's representatives, the landlord and the minister.

The populations of the north, still devout and deeply concerned with religion, gave support to the Free Church which was totally lacking in most new towns. Emigrant Gaelic communities in Canada gave support too. As far as proselytizing the factory operatives went, it was too late. The Free Church took up guardianship of the rearguard of the presbyterian position, and defended it with Scripture and with restrictions on their adherents' way of life. They tended not to marry outside their community, and were extremely intolerant of Godlessness (which they equated with the practices of any other persuasion). Teaching was of resignation to divine will, and this bred a passive attitude to civil life; often Free Kirk members did not vote. Religious melancholia became the commonest reason for admission to the new lunatic asylums of the north, ranking ahead of alcoholism. Mr Kennedy, the immensely popular Free Church minister of Dingwall, could preach, after a visit to Free Churches in America, of his feelings as he stood beside Niagara Falls that they represented the perfect picture of the endlessly flowing and unfailing wrath of God, from which Christ gave the only shelter. It was an austere doctrine.

If the Free Kirk did not make the hoped-for contribution to national life, neither did the Church of Scotland after the Disruption. The remnant clung to traditional ways for many years to come. Scotland became increasingly secular, though the passions engendered by the Disruption lived long.

Hugh Miller

Hugh Miller, born in 1802, is another characteristic Scot of his day. He was brought up by poor parents in a little fishing town, Cromarty in Ross. His career and interests had three phases: he began working as a stonemason, earning enough to give himself the leisure to read and study—though it was hard and taxing work. Quarrying in the sandstone of the Black Isle aroused his interest in the fossil fish which came to light, and he became a self-taught geologist, observing and recording fossil remains, particularly those of marine life, with great accuracy. The third phase of his career was as a journalist: a few articles were taken by the local paper, the *Inverness Courier*, and led to an introduction to Thomas Chalmers, who saw in him a powerful ally and writer on the burning topics which led to the Disruption.

Miller went to Edinburgh in 1840 as editor of the evangelical paper *The Witness*, and spent the remaining 16 years of his life working for this paper, taking a leading part in the controversies of the times, and also publishing work which he had completed earlier: *The Old Red Sandstone, Footsteps of the Creator* and *Testimony of the Rocks*, which combined original observations of fossils with his unwavering Bible-based faith. *Scenes and Legends of the North of Scotland* and *My Schools and Schoolmasters* drew on his early life, and still provide insights into his hard childhood in the north. Hugh Miller became noted, in the easy sentimental way of the mid-century, because his origins were humble and his

attainments were notable. He was often held up as a good Scots example of self-help, on the model of Samuel Smiles; though his career was unusual it fed the myth of the 'lad o' pairts' who rose through his own unaided endeavours. There were not many as original as Hugh Miller.

By the mid-century most men in Central Scotland were confident in progress and the power of the steam engine, railways were linking the major towns, and the Clyde was busy with shipbuilding and heavy engineering. Farming was prosperous in the Lowland areas. But complacency was shattered by the severe food shortages and downright famines of 'The Hungry Forties'. The Highlands were only a little less dependent than the west of Ireland was on the potato and the blight which affected the crop had dire results in the north-west and on the Islands. In the winter of 1846 public distress began to be noticeable in the north-east of Scotland too, and by the spring of 1847 severe food riots had erupted all along the coast from Wick south to Aberdeen. Hungry mobs attacked grain merchants' stores, and rioted, to the great alarm of the authorities. Newspapers carried stories of grain sacks slit open and ships' cargoes being interfered with at many Moray ports. The poor tenantry, dependent on their own potato patches, were frantic when the crop failed, and vented their fury on the grain merchants and on the large farmers who they considered—probably correctly—were forcing up prices to reap a harvest from their want. The government did not intervene directly: the free operation of a market economy had become a political tenet, though the handful of troops in Fort George were called out. A sad result of the food riots in the Moray Firth was that supplies of grain were prevented from reaching the small ports of the west Highlands, where conditions were almost as grave as they were in Ireland, due to the total failure of the potato crop and the lack of imported grain.

Gradually throughout the hungry north, piecemeal remedies and returning confidence averted worse disorders. Subsidies, soup kitchens and charity were employed with paternalistic price fixing or subsidizing of food grains in some towns, and by some large landowners. A general sympathy with the riotous poor was felt by most classes in the Highlands; this was shown by the difficulty authority had in finding special constables to swear in, or to act against mobs: passive sympathy was widespread, and eventually public opinion forced down the profiteers' prices. Queen Victoria, in the Speech from the Throne in 1847, voiced the government's attitude:

> Outrages have been repressed, as far as it was possible, by the military and the police. It is satisfactory for me to observe, that in many of the distressed districts the patience and resignation of the people has been exemplary.

Deference still ruled, but what had most satisfied the distressed was the support of their countrymen.

'From the lone sheiling . . . mountains divide us and a waste of seas'

Emigration from Scotland continued throughout the early nineteenth century to be a solution many adopted for solving their difficulties. Though some of the more affluent classes continued to migrate, often to join other Scots communities in Canada, Australia or New Zealand, the hungry mid-century years saw a great increase in the emigration of the destitute. Aided by cheap passages and emigration societies, whole families set out. This presented difficulties for the colonial authorities, who were anxious to encourage young healthy and hard-working emigrants, but were not encouraging to the elderly and infirm. Were emigrants to leave the old folks behind? And would they transplant? It was an agonizing decision, either way. Only too often the emigrants found on arrival that their close ties of kinship had to be broken because of demands of employment, which split them up. Emigration usually held a great deal of anguish. The pressures, economic and emotional, which had taken earlier generations of Scotsmen into Europe as traders or soldiers now left other waves in the new dominions, and in America where the influence of Scottish immigrants has been great. Most Scots retained a strong loyalty to their home territory, and to an increasingly imaginary Scotland, nourished by sentimental songs and the rituals of St Andrew's Nights, and by extended debates over the Disruption. Many small local papers in Scotland still owe their existence to the number of copies posted overseas to grandsons of exiles, who continue to read the small news of home.

Our Highland Journal

Queen Victoria epitomizes something of what went wrong with attitudes towards Scotland, held by both the native-born and the foreign onlooker through the later nineteenth century. The little girl who had been enthralled by the novels and poetry of Sir Walter Scott came to the throne in 1837, and a few years later made her first visit to the Highlands, with her recently married consort, Prince Albert. They stayed in noble houses, and Blair Castle, the seat of the Duke of Atholl, captivated her. Years later she was persuaded to publish *Leaves from our Highland Journal* which records some of her enthusiasms, and some of Albert's first sage reactions to Scotland. 'Glasgow,' he remarked, as they surveyed it from the Broomielaw, 'is very like Paris.' At Perth, 'Albert was charmed and said it put him in mind of Basle,' and further up the road to Blair Atholl she recorded that he said, 'the chief beauty of mountain scenery consisted in the frequent changes'. Albert, in spite of the homesickness revealed in his comments, became as enthusiastic for the Highlands of Scotland as the queen, and after some trials they

167

bought Balmoral on Deeside, which they made into the model of a royal retreat. Albert discussed the rebuilding of the castle, and the decoration; he covered the walls, chairs, curtains and carpets with many inventive new tartans of his own design. He and the royal children wore the kilt, and bearded Highland ghillies served them on bended knee.

Queen Victoria deluded herself on two counts: that she was able to lead a simple life at Balmoral, and that she understood, as she loved, the Scots who served her. She wrote about the brave manly fellows: 'All the Highlanders are so amusing and really pleasant and instructive to talk to—women as well as men— and latter so gentlemanlike.'

Leaves from Our Highland Journal sold thousands of copies over the years, and the patronizing note struck by the queen was echoed by her loyal and well-off subjects, who flocked after her to hire shooting lodges and to spend the late summer in the north. The railways brought them, with their English servants, their waggonettes and their shooting and fishing tackle. Much of Scotland degenerated into playgrounds for the rich for just a couple of months a year, and the old habits of deference became distorted into public extremes of civility which hid deep alienation on the part of the remaining inhabitants, reduced to a servile role as picturesque Highlanders, the source of pawky sayings on the stalk or at the riverside. It took the decline of shooting tenancies, among other things, to restore some sense of nationhood to Scotland.

Victorian Britain tended to overlook the busy mills and iron foundries, the jute mills of Dundee and the tweed mills of the Borders—they were necessary but not picturesque. The great majority of Scots were in industries rather than in the marginal business of ministering to shooting tenants, and they quietly got on with their labours, keeping to their old Scots traditions of hard work, democratic theological dispute, hard drinking, and a respect for education and little else. The self-education of the working classes was striking. The union movement, after a slow start, began growing in Central Scotland. But to the external eye, Scotland

was an August retreat, beginning north of Perth, where Highland games took place in the rain.

Not the final word

It is a little arbitrary to stop writing about Scotland at the midpoint of the nineteenth century, but all selective history is arbitrary. It can be argued on one hand that since the Disruption of the kirk there has been no single wholly Scottish event, unrelated to other countries and other pressures, and that the uneasy unity of Great Britain has now become a reality. Economic forces sweep across the whole world, ignoring frontiers, taking investment elsewhere and leaving men with obsolete skills. Political power still resides in Westminster, and the monarch makes visits to Scotland, and stays at Balmoral. On the other hand the Scottish nation is a green and vigorous reality, still making a peculiarly Scots contribution to the national life of Britain and, through the millions of people who claim Scots descent, to the world.

> Lourd on my hert as winter lies
> The state that Scotland's in the day,
> Spring to the North has aye come slow
> But noo dour winter's like to stay
>   For guid,
>   And no' for guid!

On Hugh MacDiarmid's cryptic note of optimism we end.

Further Reading

The Field of Thistles was written for the general reader who wants an outline of Scotland's history. Of course it is a partial, perhaps even partisan, history, and I am aware of many gaps or brief allusions to deep and interesting topics for which there was no space.

What we hope is that readers of this introduction may be encouraged to go on from this start to tackle the many excellent detailed histories of Scotland, biographies of leading citizens and accounts of industrial, social and labour movements which exist and are easy to find. A very short book list is given below; all these volumes include detailed bibliographies to encourage further reading.

Rosalind Mitchison   *A History of Scotland*, London, 1970.

T. C. Smout   *A History of the Scottish People*, 1560-1830, London, 1969.

The Edinburgh History of Scotland, 4 vols, Edinburgh.

    A. A. Duncan: *Scotland: The making of the Kingdom.*

    Ranald Nicholson: *Scotland: The Later Middle Ages.*

    Gordon Donaldson: *Scotland: James V to James VII.*

    William Ferguson: *Scotland:* 1689 to the Present.

The New History of Scotland: Edward Arnold, London, paperback (in course of completion in eight volumes).

    G. W. S. Barrow: *Kingship and Unity,* 100-1306 *AD*

    R. Mitchison: *Lordship to Patronage* 1603-1745.

    Jenny Wormald: *Court, Kirk and Community,* 1470-1625.

    Bruce Lenman: *Integration, Enlightenment and Industrialisation,* 1746-1832.

    Christopher Harvie: *No Gods and Precious Few Heroes,* 1914-1980.

(Titles not yet published are A. R. Smyth: *Warlords and Holy Men,* 500-1000 *AD*; A. GRANT: *Independence and Nationhood* 1306-1469; and S. and O. Checkland: *Industry and Ethos* 1832-1914.)

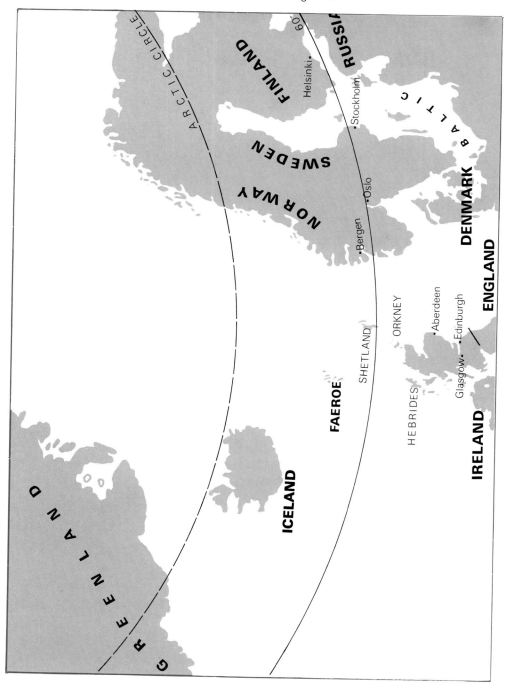

Index

175